Crossroads Café

PHOTO STORIES A

The publication of *Crossroads Café* was directed by the members of the Heinle Secondary and Adult ESL Publishing Team.

Editorial Director:	Roseanne Mendoza
Senior Production Services Coordinator:	Lisa McLaughlin
Market Development Director:	Andy Martin

Also participating in the publication of the program were:

Vice President and Publisher, ESL:	Stanley Galek
Developmental Editor:	Sally Conover
Production Editor:	Maryellen Killeen
Manufacturing Coordinator:	Mary Beth Hennebury
Full Service Design and Production:	PC&F, Inc.

Manufactured in the United States of America.

ISBN-13: 978-0-838-46608-7

ISBN-10: 0-8384-66087

11 12 13 14 15   09 08 07

Photo Credits
Episodes 1, 2, 3, 4, 5, 6, 9, 10, 13, 14, 16, 17, 18: Stanley Newton
Episodes 7, 8, 11, 12, 15, 19, 20, 21, 22, 23, 24, 25, 26: Jane O'Neal

Crossroads Café
PHOTO STORIES A

K. Lynn Savage • Patricia Mooney Gonzalez
with Edwina Hoffman

THOMSON

HEINLE

Australia Canada Mexico Singapore Spain United Kingdom United States

Acknowledgments

Rigorous review by members of the National Academic Council contributed to the initial design as well as the philosophical underpinnings of the products: Fiona Armstrong, Office of Adult and Continuing Education, New York City Board of Education; Janet Buongiorno, Adult Literacy Enhancement Center, Edison, New Jersey; Yvonne Cadiz, Adult and Community Education Program, Hillsborough County Public Schools, Florida; the late Jim Dodd, Bureau of Adult and Community Education, Department of Education, Florida; Chela Gonzalez, Metropolitan Adult Education Program, San Jose, California; Chip Harman, United States Information Agency, Washington, D.C.; Edwina Hoffman, Dade County Public Schools, Florida; Maggie Steinz, Illinois State Board of Education; Dennis Terdy, Adult Learning Resource Center, Des Plaines, Illinois; Inaam Mansour, Arlington Education and Employment Program, Arlington, Virginia; Fortune Valenty, Perth Amboy Public Schools, New Jersey; Kathleen Santopietro Weddel, Colorado Department of Education.

Collaboration among the Institute for Social Research at the University of Michigan, Interwest Applied Research in Portland, Oregon, and the National Center for Adult Literacy provided evaluation data that guided modification of student materials and development of teacher/tutor materials. Guiding and directing the evaluations were Jere Johnston, Dan Wagner, Regie Stites, and Evelyn Brzezinski. Participating pilot sites included the following: Alhambra School District, California; The Brooklyn Adult Learning Center, New York City Board of Education; Dade County Public Schools, Florida; Mt. Hood Community College, Portland, Oregon; Jewish Family Services, San Diego, California; Polish Welfare Association, Chicago, Illinois; One-Stop Immigration Center, Los Angeles, California; Even Start Program, Northside Independent School District, San Antonio, Texas; Margarita R. Huantes, Learning and Leadership Development Center, San Antonio, Texas; San Diego Community College District.

The collaboration with INTELECOM resulted in provocative stories, which provided meaningful contexts for the *Worktext's* activities. Thank you to Sarah for graciously providing whatever was needed and holding everything together during the most frenetic stages of the project; Peter and Glenn for providing entertaining and relevant story lines; Bob for keeping everyone properly focused; and Sally, for her leadership as well as her commitment and involvement in all aspects of the project.

Extensive experience of Heinle & Heinle and its staff in publishing language-learning materials ensured quality print materials. The authors wish to thank Nancy Mann, *Worktexts* editor, for her professionalism and expertise; Sally Conover, *Photo Stories* editor, for the dedication, patience, and attention to detail that the Photo Stories required; Lisa McLaughlin, production coordinator, for ensuring that the extremely tight production schedule was met without sacrificing quality; Maryellen Killeen, production editor, for her infinite patience and good humor in sorting through the hundreds of photos for the Photo Stories; Roseanne Mendoza, acquisitions editor, for her willingness to take the risks that the development of cutting edge products requires and for her commitment to fighting for the things she believes in.

Table of Contents

Photo Story A

SCANS* AT-A-GLAN

Video Time (min: sec) Worktext	Crossroads Café Lesson Plans	SCANS Discussion Focus
1 Opening Day		
• 3:03–4:33 • 11:45–14:13 Text p. 13 • Text p. 12	• Applying for the café food server job • Culture Clip: Finding and Interviewing for Jobs • What Do You Think?	• Information: *evaluate data* • Systems: *understand social systems, monitor and correct performance* • Thinking: *think creatively* and *make decisions*
2 Growing Pains		
• 3:59–5:55 16:58–18:13 • Text p. 26	• Henry's working predicament • What Do You Think?	• Personal Qualities: *choose ethical courses of action* • Interpersonal: *negotiate*
3 Worlds Apart		
• 12:08–13:56 21:14–23:03 • Text p. 40	• Different cultures, different expectations • What Do You Think?	• Systems: *design* and *understand social systems* • Interpersonal: *work with people from culturally diverse backgrounds*
4 Who's the Boss?		
• 7:54–10:26 21:26–23:02 • Text p. 54	• Jamal's lesson about lying and integrity • What Do You Think?	• Personal Qualities: *believe in own self-worth, choose right thing to do* • Information: *acquire and evaluate*
• 14:39–16:18 Text p. 55	• Culture Clip: Career Changes	• Systems: *understand organizational systems* • Information: *analyze and communicate*
5 Lost and Found		
• 6:07–8:07 • 12:55–13:51	• Disruptive behavior in the workplace • A solution to disruptive behavior	• Human Resources: *evaluate performance, provide feedback* • Interpersonal Skills: *teach others new skills*
• 17:53–19:37 Text p. 69 • Text p. 68	• Culture Clip: Neighbors form groups to prevent crime • What Do You Think?	• Systems: *understand and operate effectively within systems* • Information: *interpret and communicate*
6 Time Is Money		

• 10:00–11:59
 	
• Text pp. 80–81
	• Recommendations about efficiency and organization in the workplace
	
	• Read and Write
		• Information: *organize and maintain information*
		  Systems: *monitor and correct performance*
		  Thinking: *solve problems*
		• Information: *organize*

• 12:09–14:21 Text p. 83	• Culture Clip: Time is important in the U.S.	• Resources: *allocate time*
• 15:50–17:48 • Text p. 82	• Different opinions about money and people • What Do You Think?	• Information: *interpret and communicate* • Interpersonal: *communicate ideas to justify position*
7 Fish Out of Water		
• 11:44–13:39 • Text p. 96	• Different opinions about cultural pride • What Do You Think?	• Personal Qualities: *believe in own self-worth* • Interpersonal: *persuade and convince others*

*SCANS is an acronym for the Secretary's Commission on Achieving Necessary Skills (U.S. Department of Labor, 1991)

Video Time (min: sec) Worktext	Crossroads Café Lesson Plans	SCANS Discussion Focus
8 Family Matters		
• 15:15–17:35 • 9:29–11:59 Text p. 111	• Single-parent challenges in working • Culture Clip: Single Parenting	• Thinking: *solve problems* • Interpersonal: *persuade and convince others*
9 Rush to Judgment		
• 4:14–5:54 • 21:26–23:12 • Text p. 124	• Police mistake Jamal for burglar • Brashov vouches for Jamal • What Do You Think?	• Systems: *understand organizational systems* • Information: *analyze and communicate* • Thinking: *draw conclusions*
• 6:24–8:48 Text p. 125	• Culture Clip: Roles of a Police Officer	• Information: *acquire and evaluate*
10 Let the Buyer Beware		
• 4:37–7:07 • 8:02–9:37 • Text p. 138	• New customer charms Brashov • Brashov falls for scam • What Do You Think?	• Thinking: *draw conclusions* • Information: *acquire, evaluate* • Information: *analyze and communicate*
• 17:58–19:59 Text p. 139	• Culture Clip: Consumer Scams	• Information: *acquire and evaluate, analyze and communicate* • Thinking: *draw conclusions*
11 No Vacancy		
• 5:09–6:22 8:25–10:19 • Text p. 152	• Recognizing discrimination • What Do You Think?	• Personal Qualities: *integrity* Interpersonal: *work with people of diverse backgrounds* • Information: *acquire and evaluate*
• 20:16–22:10 • 13:16–16:46 Text p. 153	• Documenting discrimination • Culture Clip: Discrimination	• Thinking: *recognize problem, create and complete a plan of action* • Information: *interpret and communicate*
12 Turning Points		
• 10:06–11:48 22:32–23:42 • Text p. 166	• Café vandalism foiled • What Do You Think?	• Thinking: *choose best alternative based on facts* Systems: *work within the system* • Information: *acquire and evaluate, analyze and communicate*
13 Trading Places		
• 9:42–11:14 • 17:58–19:40 • Text p. 180	• Café employees trade places • Difficulty of trading places • What Do You Think?	• Resources: *use facilities and materials* Systems: *develop alternative system, monitor and correct performance* • Thinking: *use efficient learning techniques* • Information: *analyze and communicate*
• 21:54–23:47 • 6:46–9:35 Text p. 181	• Resolving an argument • Culture Clip: The Roles Couples Choose	• Personal Qualities: *self esteem, self management* Interpersonal: *negotiate* • Thinking: *solve problems*

To the Learner: About *Crossroads Café*

These pages explain what the *Crossroads Café* program is and how to use it. If you have problems understanding these explanations, ask someone to read and discuss them with you. If you start with a clear idea of how to use *Crossroads Café* correctly, your chances for success will be great.

Crossroads Café provides a unique method to learn English. The use of a television series and videos will help you improve your English. The *Crossroads Café* books are excellent tools for helping you use the television series or the videos to improve your listening, speaking, reading, and writing in English. The next section explains how each piece of the program can help you. It also answers some important questions about the series and how it should be used.

What Is *Crossroads Café?*

Crossroads Café is a course for studying English. The course teaches English as it entertains. It also helps you understand North American culture and use that understanding to live and work in the culture more successfully.

What Are the Parts of the Program?

There are three parts of the program for learners.
- The 26 television programs or the videos
- The two *Photo Stories* books
- The two *Worktexts*

You will use television programs or videos with the *Photo Stories,* the *Worktexts,* or both to learn English.

What Are the Television Programs?

The television programs are the most important part of the *Crossroads Café* program. There are 26 thirty-minute episodes that tell the story of a group of hard-working, determined people whose lives come together at a small neighborhood restaurant called Crossroads Café. Some of them are newcomers to the United States. Others have families that have been here for one or many generations. These people slowly create a successful neighborhood restaurant. During the 26 episodes, *Crossroads Café* tells of the successes and the failures, the joys and the sadness, and especially the learning experiences of the owner of the café, the people who work in it, their families, friends, acquaintances, neighbors, and the people they must cooperate with to be successful in their work and in their lives. The story is sometimes funny, sometimes sad, but always entertaining. The large picture above shows the six main characters in *Crossroads Café*. The smaller pictures around it show the characters in their lives outside the café.

These are the people you will learn about in *Crossroads Café*. You will be able to understand many of the problems they face and share many of their feelings. You will learn from their experiences—learn English and learn something about North American culture. You will also discover new ways to learn—which can be new paths to success for you in an English-speaking culture.

Most of each thirty-minute program deals with the story of the café and its six characters. But there are two other pieces in each episode that are especially good for people who want to learn English and understand North American culture. In every episode, there is a short section called "Word Play." "Word Play" always shows and explains some special way English is used in that episode. It combines cartoons, illustrations, and scenes from the episode to teach how to use English for a special purpose. For example, "Word Play" presents ways to ask for help, make suggestions, or, as this picture shows, make complaints.

The second special section that is part of every episode is the "Culture Clip." It helps you understand North American culture. You can agree or disagree with the behavior the "Culture Clip" shows, but this section will always help you think about your ideas on culture, in your own country and in your life today. This can help you understand and deal with cultural differences.

How Do I Use the Television Programs or Videos?

You can use the program if you are any of these types of learner. Here's how each type can best use the television programs or the videos.

1. **The Independent Learner.** You want to study the language on your own—possibly with the help of a tutor, a friend, a neighbor, or a family member. You may have seen an episode of *Crossroads Café* on television, or you may have heard about it from someone else—a friend or a family member. You may have seen ads for the program in a store or a library. You ordered the *Crossroads Café* program on your own because you wanted to learn English at home, by yourself or with someone else.

2. **The Distant Learner.** You study in a distance-learning program in a school. You may talk to or see your teacher once a week, once every two weeks, or once a month. But most of your study will be done alone, using the *Crossroads Café* materials. Your teacher may tell you to watch *Crossroads Café* one or more times each week and do the activities in the *Worktexts*, the *Photo Stories,* or both. When you meet with your teacher—and perhaps with other students too—you will talk about what you saw and learned. You may also do some activities from the *Teacher's Resource Book* with the other students and your teacher.

3. The Classroom Learner. You study in a regular class with a teacher in a school. You will use the *Crossroads Café* books—*Worktexts, Photo Stories,* or both—in your class. Your teacher will ask you to watch *Crossroads Café* programs and do some of the activities in your book at home. In class, you will work with other students to do more activities in the *Worktext* or the *Photo Stories* and other activities from the *Teacher's Resource Book.* Your teacher may also show important pieces of the episodes again in class and discuss them with the students.

How Do I Use the *Worktexts?*

Each of the two *Crossroads Café Worktexts* contains thirteen episodes—half the episodes in the complete series. Every *Worktext* lesson has the same parts, which you will use to practice and improve your English before and after you watch the television or video.

The *Worktexts* are carefully written to help learners at three different levels of English study—high beginning, low intermediate, and high intermediate. You can "grow" with the program by using the same *Worktexts* and videos over and over as you acquire more English. Here's how these multi-level *Worktexts* can work for you.

The different activities in each section of the books are marked with colored stars—one, two, or three stars for the three different levels of learners. Here are two possible ways to use the *Worktexts.*

1. If you are working alone, without a teacher, try to work through all three levels in the first unit to see which level suits you best. Be honest with yourself. If you check your answers and see that you've made mistakes at a certain level, it's best to choose the level below that one. If you have a teacher or a tutor, he or she will probably choose a level for you. After you know your level, always do the activities for that level, as well as the activities for the levels before it. For example, let's say you decide you are a two-star learner. In every section, you will do the one-star activity first and then the two-star activity. If you are a three-star learner, you will do the one-star and the two-star activities before you do the three-star activity. Don't skip the lower-level activities. They are the warm-up practice that can help you succeed when you reach your own level.

2. In each section, go as far as you can in the star system. For example, in the first activity in an episode, you may be able to do both the one-star and the two-star activities easily. However, you may not be able to complete the three-star activity. So, stop after the two-star activity and move on to the next section. In the second section, you may be able to all three levels of stars easily, or you may only be able to do the one-star activity. Always begin with the one-star activity and, if you succeed, then move on to the more advanced activities. If you have problems with an activity, get help right away from your teacher or tutor, or from someone whose English is better than yours.

Remember, if you are studying alone you can choose one of those two ways of working. If you have a teacher or a tutor, that person can help you decide how to work. But if you have problems with any activity, always try to get help immediately from your teacher, your tutor, or someone else who knows more English than you. That way, you can understand what to do and how to correct yourself.

How Can the *Worktext* Activities Help Me Learn?

The *Worktext* activities do three things:

1. They help you understand the story on the video.
2. They provide language practice.
3. They ask you to think about, talk about, and write about your ideas.

Understanding the Story: To help you understand the story, the *Worktext* has activities for you to do before and after you watch the episode.

Before you watch, you can do three things:

- Look at the big picture on the first page for the episode. Look at the title. Then try to guess what the story is about. Talk about your ideas with someone.

- Then look at the six pictures in the "Before You Watch" section. Talk about the pictures with someone. Do the exercises that go with the pictures. Check your answers by looking at the answer key in the back of the book.

- Finally, read the questions in the "Focus for Watching" section. If you do not understand some words, use your dictionary, or ask someone what the words mean.

After you watch the episode, turn to the "After You Watch" activities in your *Worktext*. In these activities, you will do two things:

- You will match key people from the story with the focus questions.

- You will answer questions about important parts of the story and then you will put those parts in order.

Practicing the Language helps you develop your English language skills. This section of the *Worktext* gives you special activities to do after you watch the television or video. These next three sections will help you improve your grammar, your reading, and your writing.

Your New Language presents grammar for a special purpose. For example, you will learn to use commands to tell someone to do something. Or you will learn to use *can* and *know how to* to talk about what you are able to do. Here is a good way to do these activities:

- Watch "Word Play" on the video again, if possible.

- Complete the "Your New Language" section of your *Worktext*.

- Check your answers. Use the "Answer Key" in the back of the *Worktexts*.

- Practice the conversations in "Your New Language" with someone.

In Your Community presents the kind of reading you find in your everyday life. Here is a good way to do these activities:

- Answer the questions about the reading.
- Check your answers. Use the "Answer Key" in the back of your *Worktext*.
- Look for the same kind of reading in the town or city where you live.
- Compare the reading you find with the one in the *Worktext*.

Read and Write presents something that a person in *Crossroads Café* wrote. It may be a letter, a note, a diary page, or a newspaper article. Here is a good way to do these activities:

- Answer the questions about the main ideas of the writing.
- Guess the meaning of the words in the vocabulary exercises.
- Use your experiences to write about something similar.
- Share your writing with someone.

Two sections of each *Worktext* unit have exercises that ask you to give your opinions about something that happened in the story. These sections are called "What Do You Think?" and "Culture Clip."

Here is a good way to work through the **What Do You Think?** activities:

- Think about things people in the story have done or opinions they have expressed.
- Share your ideas with someone.

Here is a good way to work through the **Culture Clip** activities:

- Watch the "Culture Clip" on the video again, if possible.
- Identify the main ideas from the "Culture Clip."
- Give your own opinion about a situation related to the "Culture Clip."

Check Your English is the last activity in each unit. It is a review of vocabulary, grammar, and reading. You can check your answers with the "Answer Key" in the back of your *Worktext*.

What Are the *Photo Stories?*

The *Crossroads Café Photo Stories* do these things:

- They help you understand the story before you watch the video.
- They ask you questions to help you understand parts of the story.
- They help you improve your vocabulary.
- They help you review after you watch.

The *Photo Stories* can help you if you know a little English or a lot of English:

- They can be special books for beginning learners of English. Learners study the pictures from the video. These pictures have the words from the story in them. This combination of words and photos makes learning English easy. If you speak Spanish, you may have read *fotonovelas,* or *telefotonovelas.* The *Photo Stories* look very much like those books, and they tell interesting stories, too.

• They are also for more advanced students of English. They can be an extra help for you if you are using the *Worktexts.* You can use the *Photo Story* to preview each television or video episode. First read the *Photo Story* and then do the exercises. Then, when you watch the episode, you will be prepared to understand what is happening and know what the characters will say.

This sample page shows how the *Photo Stories* tell the story of the video and help you read to find the meaning.

This sample page shows one type of activity you will do after you read the story.

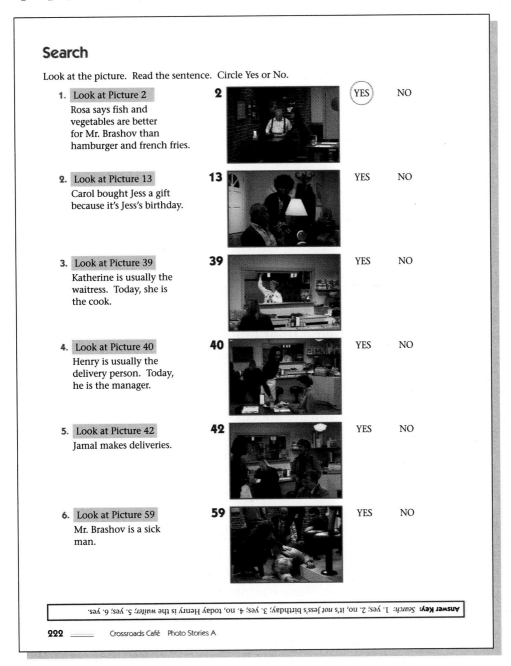

222 _____ Crossroads Café Photo Stories A

Special Questions about *Crossroads Café*

Learners of English and their teachers and tutors sometimes ask these questions about *Crossroads Café*.

What if I can't understand everything in the television or video episodes? Don't worry if you can't understand some language in the episodes. Even if you don't understand a lot of language, you can still learn from watching. You will often be able to guess what is happening in the story. This is because sometimes the people use actions that help you understand the meaning of their words. Also, sometimes they will look happy, surprised, or even angry when they speak. These facial expressions help you guess what they are saying. Learn to watch for these clues. They can help you understand the story. Good language learners know how to use these clues to help themselves. With *Crossroads Café*, you will learn to develop successful language-learning habits.

What if I can't understand the way some of the characters speak? In *Crossroads Café*, several important characters were either born in the U.S. or arrived when they were very young. They speak English without accents:

- Katherine is from the Midwest.
- Jess is from the South.
- Henry was born in China, but immigrated to the U.S. before he started school.

But some characters are from other parts of the world:

- Mr. Brashov is from Eastern Europe.
- Rosa was born in the U.S., but she grew up in Latin America.
- Jamal is from the Middle East.

These characters, like you, are still improving their English pronunciation, although they always use correct grammar. It will help you to hear many different pronunciations of English. In North America, and in the world in general, people speak English in many different ways. In schools, at work, and in the streets, other people need to understand them to communicate successfully with them. Becoming accustomed to hearing speakers from different cultures and different ethnic groups is a skill successful English speakers need to develop in our modern world.

What if the English is too fast for me? In *Crossroads Café*, the characters speak at a natural speed. Their speech is not artificially slow. In the real world, very few people talk slowly to help learners of English, so in *Crossroads Café* you will hear English spoken naturally. This will be helpful to you in the long run. But the *Crossroads Café* course can give you extra help as you become accustomed to hearing English at a normal pace. Here are four ways you can use the program to get this help:

- You can preview and review the story by using the *Photo Stories,* the *Worktext,* or both.
- If you meet with your teacher and your class, your teacher may use the video version to show again some important pieces of the episode you already watched.
- Your teacher may also show some pieces of a video episode *before* you see the complete episode at home on television.
- You can record complete episodes of *Crossroads Café* with a VCR and then play them back for yourself again and again. Or you may want to buy some or all of the video episodes by calling 1-800-ESL-BY-TV (1-800-375-2988) or 1-800-354-9706.

Why should I have a study partner? Learning a language means learning to communicate with others. Using videos and television programs to learn a language has many advantages, but seeing the programs and doing the reading, writing, and thinking activities in the *Worktext* is not enough. Having a study partner gives you the opportunity to practice your new language skills. That person can be another *Crossroads Café* English learner. It can be a wonderful shared experience to do the lessons and watch the videos with a partner who is also learning English. But your partner could also be someone who knows more English than you do. It can be someone who is not studying with the *Crossroads Café* materials—someone like a relative who knows English and can help you—perhaps a son or a daughter, a husband or a wife, or any other family member. Or the partner can be a neighbor, a person who works with you, a friend, or any person who knows more English than you do. And, finally, the partner can be a formal or informal tutor—a librarian, a high-school student, or someone who used to be a teacher. Any of these people can help make the time you spend learning English more productive. If your partner knows more English than you do, he or she can use the *Crossroads Café Partner Guide*. The *Partner Guide* is small and easy to use, but they have some excellent ideas for helping learners of English.

1 Opening Day

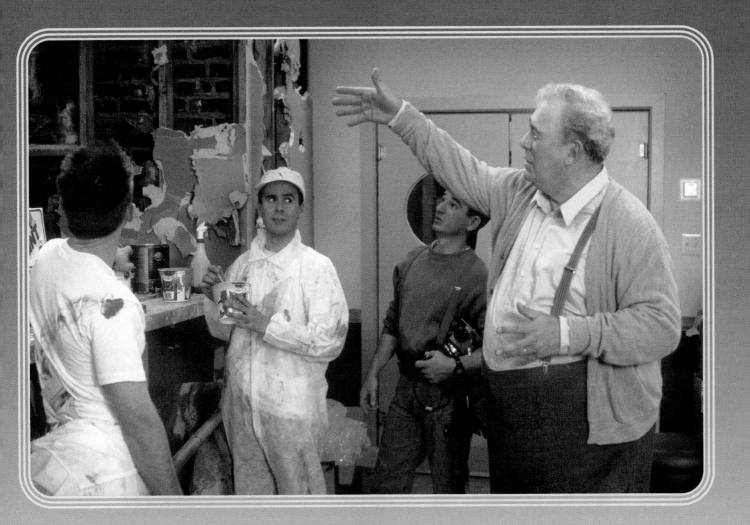

Meet Victor Brashov. He is opening
a new restaurant.

What does he need to do?

Who's in This Story?

Victor Brashov
the café owner

Jamal Al-Jibali
an unemployed engineer
the handyman

a sign painter

Katherine Blake
a job applicant

Rosa Rivera
a job applicant

Henry Chang
a high school student

Jess Washington
a retired postal worker

1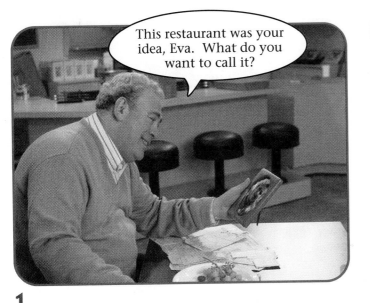

This restaurant was your idea, Eva. What do you want to call it?

2

Mr. Brashov has a problem.

You don't know what you're doing.

I know I'm opening the restaurant in two days.

3

Find another cook!

4

What are you going to call this place?

I don't know. That is another problem. My chef just quit!

5

A woman applies for a job.

6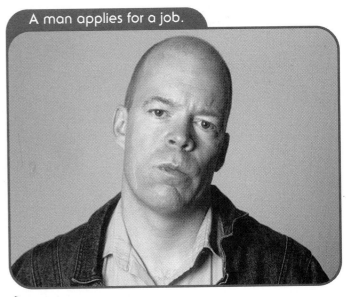

A man applies for a job.

Another applicant comes.

Hello, I am Katherine Blake. The employment office sent me.

7

Here's my resume.

8

I am looking for Mr. Brashov.

I am Mr. Brashov. Who are you?

9

I am Rosa Rivera. I am here for the waitress job.

10

I am interviewing for that job.

I had an appointment.

11

✓ **Check Yourself**

1. Who quits?
   a. the chef
   b. Katherine Blake

2. What job do Rosa and Katherine want?
   a. the cook job
   b. the waitress job

12

13

14

15

16

17

18

Mr. Brashov still has problems.

I am ready for the name of the restaurant, Mr. Brashov.

When I think of a name I will tell you.

Mr. Brashov, the waitress job?

19

✓ **Check Yourself**

3. What does Rosa show Mr. Brashov?
   a. that she can wait tables
   b. that she can cook

4. What does the sign painter want from Mr. Brashov?
   a. the name of the cook
   b. the name of the restaurant

20

Katherine and Rosa talk at the same time.

21

This is one of my desserts. Try it!

No thank you. I need someone who can cook, not start fires.

22

Rosa is very angry and says something in Spanish.

23

Is this a good time to tell you about . . .

Wait!

24

25

26

27

28

29

30

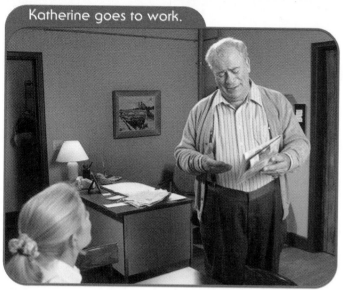

31 Katherine goes to work.

32 Hello, this is Katherine. What would you like us to deliver?

33 A teenager enters the restaurant.

Can I help you?

I am trying to find the post office.

34 Go to the corner and turn right.

O.K.

35 A few minutes later the teenager returns.

That was fast.

I got a little lost.

Here is one burger to go.

36 You go to the corner and turn right.

Oh, I thought you said left!

37

38

39

40

✓ Check Yourself

7. Why does Henry come to the restaurant?

  a. because he is hungry

  b. because he is lost

8. What does Mr. Brashov ask Henry to do?

  a. to deliver some food

  b. to clean the tables

41

42

43 Henry returns, and Mr. Brashov pays him.

Here you are. Thank you very much.

Thank you.

44 An older man enters the restaurant.

45

Hello. My name is Jess Washington.

I am Victor Brashov.

What do you do for a living?

I am retired. I like to read and play chess.

46

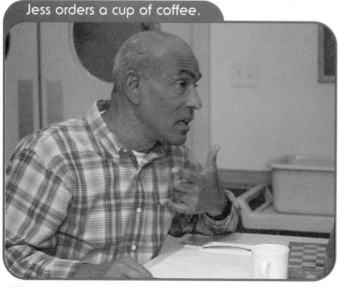

47 Jess orders a cup of coffee.

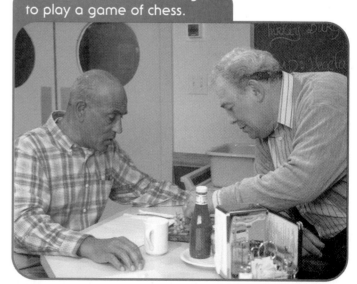

48 Mr. Brashov and Jess begin to play a game of chess.

49

50

51

52

53

54

55

56

57

58

59

60

Tell the Story

Match the picture with the sentence. Then tell the story.

1.

2.

3.

4.

5.

6.

a. Mr. Brashov hires a waitress.

b. Jamal, the handyman, helps Mr. Brashov.

c. Mr. Brashov is opening a restaurant.

d. A customer, Jess, gives the café a name.

e. Mr. Brashov hires a cook.

f. He asks a teenager with a bicycle to deliver food.

Search

For each sentence in the box, write the number in a circle.

1. Mr. Brashov's restaurant has no name.

2. Jess suggests a name for the restaurant.

3. The chef quits.

4. Mr. Brashov hires a cook.

5. Mr. Brashov doesn't hire the first applicants.

6. Mr. Brashov hires a waitress.

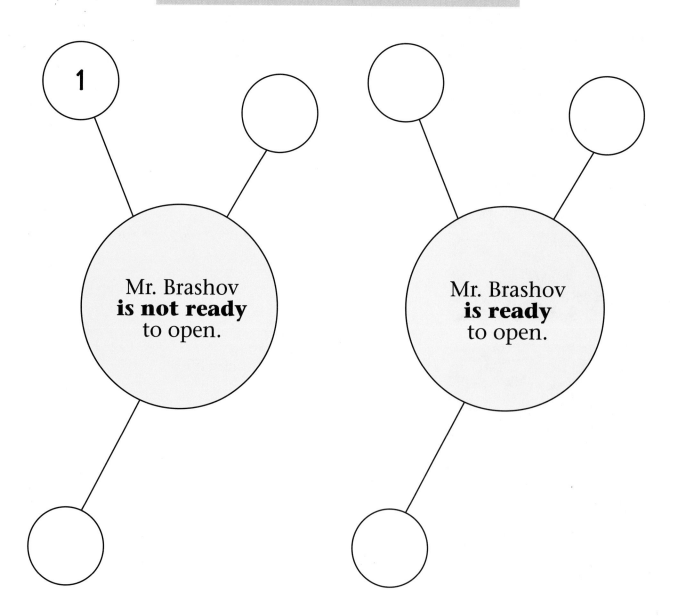

Build Your Vocabulary

Rosa's Dessert

Read the words in the list. Find the numbers in the picture.

1. ladder
2. ceiling light
3. water pitcher
4. fire extinguisher
5. fire
6. pan
7. cart
8. oven mitt
9. apron

Complete the sentences. Use the words from the picture.

1. The pan handle is hot, so Rosa is wearing an ___oven mitt (8)___.

2. Rosa is pushing a _____.

3. There is a tall _____ behind Mr. Brashov.

4. Jamal thinks that Rosa's dessert is a _____.

5. Rosa is wearing an _____ to keep her dress clean.

6. I can't see the top of the ladder because of the _____.

7. A dessert and a _____ are on the cart.

8. Katherine is pouring water from the _____ to put out the fire.

9. Mr. Brashov has a _____ in his hand.

Picture Dictionary

Study the picture and the English word. Copy the word. Then you may write the word in your language.

1.

burn down

b u r n   d o w n

_____

my language

2.

chess

— — — — —

_____

3.

cook

— — — —

_____

4.

desserts

— — — — — — — —

_____

5.

deliver

— — — — — — —

_____

6.

deliver

— — — — — — —

_____

7.

form

— — — —

_____

8.

handyman

— — — — — — — —

_____

9.

waitress

— — — — — — — —

_____

Glossary

appointment: a time to meet with someone. *My appointment with the dentist is at 4:00 today.*

employment office: a place that joins companies that need workers with people who need jobs. *I got this job through an employment office.*

interview: ask questions to find out information. *She gave good answers to the questions in her interview.*

quit: to stop. *I quit because I didn't like the job.*

teenager: someone who is between 13 and 19 years old. *Teenagers like to be free.*

Growing Pains

An inspector looks at Mr. Brashov's new restaurant. Henry's parents listen to Henry's new ideas. These are new experiences for Mr. Brashov and Henry.

Why are the new experiences difficult?

Who's in This Story?

Ms. Reilly
an inspector from the Department
of Health and Safety

Victor Brashov
the café owner

Henry

Uncle Fred

Edward
Henry's
brother

Mrs. Chang

Mr. Chang

Grandpa
Chang

Grandma
Chang

The Chang Family

Jamal
the handyman

Katherine
the waitress

Rosa
the cook

Jess
a regular customer

1 It's late in the day at Crossroads Café.

One for lunch?

No, I'm looking for the owner.

2 What can I do for you?

Are you the owner?

Yes, I am Victor Brashov.

Margaret Reilly. Inspector.

3 I am here to inspect the restaurant.

For what?

Violations.

4 Please direct me to the supply room.

Please follow me.

5 A man enters the restaurant.

Lunch?

I'd like to order pie to go.

6 Have a seat. I'll have your pie in a minute.

Thank you.

7

8

9

10

11

12

13

14

15

16

17

18

19

How do you do.

Nice to meet you.

20

I work here, Uncle Fred.

So you're making extra money!

21

Henry's Uncle Fred leaves, and Ms. Reilly enters from the kitchen.

Are we going to pass the inspection?

You'll find out when you read my report.

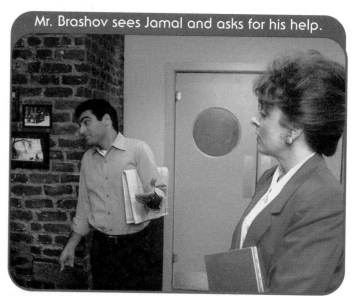

22

Well, it was nice to meet you.

Mr. Brashov, I am not finished. I need to inspect your office, the bathrooms, the kitchen.

23

Who is going to show me around?

Katherine? Rosa?

I have to plan tomorrow's menu.

I have to pick up my children.

24

Mr. Brashov sees Jamal and asks for his help.

Check Yourself

3. Who is surprised to see Henry?
   a. Inspector Reilly
   b. Uncle Fred

4. What does Henry want to tell Mr. Brashov?
   a. that his parents don't know he is working
   b. that his parents are happy he is working

31

32

33

34

35

36

37

38

39

41

40

✓ **Check Yourself**

5. How do Henry's parents feel about his job?
   a. They are happy about it.
   b. They aren't happy about it.

6. Why does Henry want to work?
   a. because he wants to buy things
   b. because he doesn't like school

42

43

> Do you know what's in this? It is toxic.

44

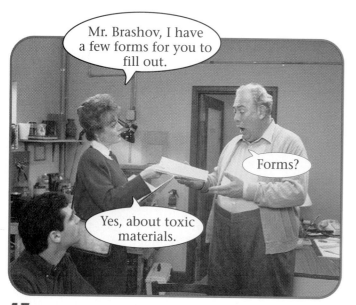

45

> Mr. Brashov, I have a few forms for you to fill out.

> Forms?

> Yes, about toxic materials.

Mr. Brashov returns to the dining area and greets customers.

46

> Hello. Right this way, please.

Henry is surprised to see his parents.

47

48

> What are you doing here?

> Do you know each other?

49

50

51

52

53

54

55 "I was afraid to show it to you. I didn't think you would sign it."

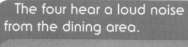

56 "This form is a lie. It means nothing."

✔ **Check Yourself**

7. Why do Mr. and Mrs. Chang go to Crossroads Café?

   a. They want to try Rosa's cooking.

   b. They want to see where Henry works.

8. Who signed the permission form for Henry to work?

   a. Mr. and Mrs. Chang

   b. Henry or one of his friends

57

The four hear a loud noise from the dining area.

58

59 "Rosa, what was that noise?" "Ms. Reilly fell."

60 "Mr. Brashov, what is this?" "a violin case"

61

I fell over it.

Does that violate any rules?

62

Ms. Reilly leaves.

Mr. Brashov, I'm sorry about the violin case. I have a lesson later today.

It's all right.

63

Henry, are you still practicing the violin?

Sure.

We thought you were only interested in earning money.

I never said that.

Maybe we were wrong about some things.

64

65

Mr. Brashov, do you have any more copies of that form?

Are you going to sign it?

First you show us you can work here, do your school work, and continue your violin lessons.

66

Late afternoon two weeks later at Crossroads Café, Mr. Brashov is opening the mail.

Oh, oh.

What is it?

The report from that inspector.

Mr. Brashov reads the form.

Crossroads Café passed the inspection.

Congratulations.

67

Aach! Ms. Reilly is coming back sometime in the next 3 months.

That's bad.

68

Henry, this might interest you. Your parents signed the work-study form.

69

70

Henry practices his violin.

71

✔ **Check Yourself**

9. What does Mrs. Reilly's report say?

   a. Crossroads Café passed the inspection.

   b. Crossroads Café didn't pass the inspection.

10. Why do Mr. and Mrs. Chang decide Henry can work?

   a. because he is still practicing the violin

   b. because he is earning money

72

Tell the Story

Put the pictures and sentences in order. Number 1 to 8. Then tell the story to someone.

____ a.

Mrs. Chang finds out Henry has a job.

____ b.

Rosa finds out Henry's parents don't know he works.

____ c.

Henry tells his parents he still practices the violin.

__1__ d.

Henry hides from his Uncle Fred.

____ e.

Mr. Chang says he never signed the form.

____ f.

Henry learns his parents signed the work-study form.

____ g.

Henry tries to tell Mr. Brashov his parents don't know he works.

____ h.

Henry's parents visit Crossroads Café and meet Mr. Brashov.

Search

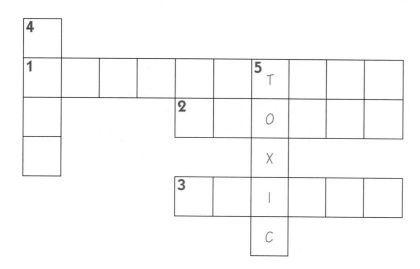

Complete the sentences. Then finish the puzzle above.

Across

1. Crossroads Café passed the ___ ___ ___ ___ ___ ___ ___ ___ ___ ___.
2. Henry's parents want Henry to practice the ___ ___ ___ ___ ___ ___.
3. Henry wants to earn money to buy a ___ ___ ___ ___ ___ ___.

Down

4. To work, Henry needs his parents to ___ ___ ___ ___ a form.
5. Mrs. Reilly found something that is _t_ _o_ _x_ _i_ _c_.

Build Your Vocabulary

Edward's Birthday Party

Read the words in the list. Find the numbers in the picture.

1. match
2. candles
3. cake
4. candlestick holders
5. presents
6. vase
7. flowers
8. bow

Complete the sentences. Use the words from the picture.

1. Everybody is looking at Edward's _____ *cake (3)* _____.

2. There are three _____ on the table.

3. There is a big _____ on two presents.

4. Mrs. Chang has a _____ in her hand.

5. She is going to light the _____ on the birthday cake.

6. Two candles are in _____.

7. There is a _____ between the candles.

8. There are some _____ in the vase.

Picture Dictionary

Study the picture and the English word. Copy the word. Then you may write the word in your language.

1.

fall

f a l l

my language

2.

guitar

_ _ _ _ _

3.

hide

_ _ _ _

4.

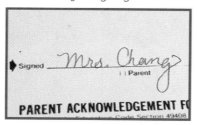

signature

_ _ _ _ _ _ _ _ _

5.

toxic

_ _ _ _ _

6.

violin

_ _ _ _ _ _

7.

violin case

_ _ _ _ _ _ _ _ _ _

8.

whisper

_ _ _ _ _ _ _

Glossary

inspect: to look at something closely. *Please inspect this bill. I don't think it is correct.*

inspection: examination. *His inspection of the building was very complete.*

inspector: a person who looks for problems. *City inspectors look at electricity and plumbing in new buildings.*

lie: not the truth. *She told a lie about her age. She isn't 39. She's 45.*

mistake: something wrong. *You made a mistake on my bill. It isn't $5.50. It's $4.50.*

report: official written information. *Her report was so good her boss promoted her.*

violations: not following rules. *I got a ticket for a parking violation. I parked next to a fire hydrant.*

3 Worlds Apart

Rosa's boyfriend Miguel comes to visit
from Mexico. He finds that Rosa is different.
They want different things.

How are Rosa and Miguel different?

Who's in This Story?

Rosa Rivera
the café cook

Miguel Sanchez
Rosa's boyfriend from Mexico

Mrs. Gilroy
a customer at the café

Carrie
Rosa's roommate

Victor Brashov
the café owner

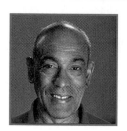

Jess
a regular customer

Henry
the busboy

Katherine
the waitress

Jamal
the handyman

1

2

3

4

5

6

7

8

9

10

✓ **Check Yourself**

1. Miguel Sanchez is
   a. from the States
   b. visiting the States

2. Miguel gives Rosa
   a. a necklace
   b. a book

11

12

Carrie practices her Spanish.

Oh, Carrie. This is Miguel. Miguel, this is my roommate, Carrie.

Hola, Miguel, cómo está?

13

Good evening, Carrie. I am feeling . . . on top of the world.

Do you want to sit down?

I can't. I have a date.

14

Carrie leaves and Rosa takes Miguel to the kitchen.

I have a little surprise for you, also. It's made with tomatoes . . . mushrooms . . . chicken.

Rosa . . . will you marry me?

15

Rosa is surprised.

I didn't think you would ask me now.

I don't want us to be apart.

16

There are many things I want to do. Miguel, I want to open a restaurant.

That's wonderful

Yes, but in this country . . .

17

Would you move here?

Rosa, Puebla is our home.

But I don't want to give up what I have here.

18

19

20

21

22

23

24

Later that night, the doorbell rings at Rosa's apartment.

25

Hello, Rosa

Hi. Thank you. They're beautiful.

26

How was work today?

I was very tired. I was up late last night.

27

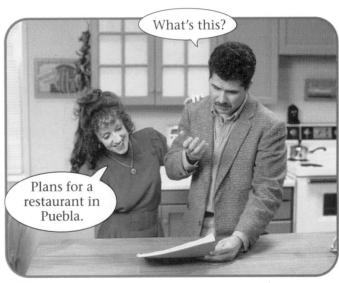

What's this?

Plans for a restaurant in Puebla.

28

Rosa . . . this is wonderful.

Here, let me show you.

29

These are some menu ideas. I want to serve food from around the world.

Hmm . . . I don't know if an international restaurant will be a success in Puebla.

30

31

32

33

34

35

36

37

Victor needs sleep. I'm surprised he can remember his own name.

He should see a doctor.

38

Katherine receives a telephone call from her daughter's school.

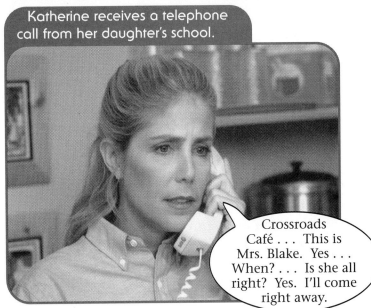

Crossroads Café . . . This is Mrs. Blake. Yes . . . When? . . . Is she all right? Yes. I'll come right away.

39

Rosa! Suzanne's in the emergency room. She fell at school. I have to go. Can you manage the lunch hour?

Don't worry. Just go!

40

Henry, I am glad you're here. Come on. We have to work fast.

41

Mrs. Gilroy arrives at the restaurant.

Excuse me. Is Mr. Brashov here?

We talked to him about a group meeting for lunch today.

A group? Just a second.

42

Hello, ladies.

Hello, Rosa. We made reservations.

43

44

45

46

47

48

49

Good job, Rosa. I just wish I could remember what I wanted to tell you.

50

That night at Rosa's apartment . . .

51

Hello, Rosa.

Hi.

52

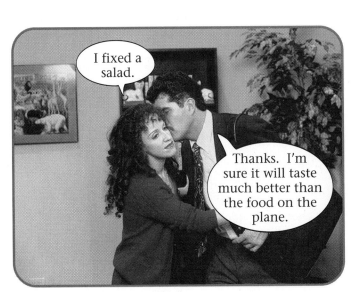

I fixed a salad.

Thanks. I'm sure it will taste much better than the food on the plane.

53

Rosita . . . I want to marry you. I don't want your plans for a restaurant to change that.

Miguel, last night wasn't about the restaurant. It was about us. We live in two very different worlds.

54

55

56

57

58

59

60

Tell the Story

Put the pictures and sentences in order. Number 1 to 5. Then tell the story to someone.

___ **a.**

Miguel tells Rosa she is different.

___ **b.**

Miguel gives Rosa a necklace.

___ **c.**

Miguel doesn't think Rosa's restaurant will be successful.

<u>1</u> **d.**

Miguel comes to visit Rosa.

___ **e.**

Rosa shows Miguel her plans.

Search

Look at the picture. Read the sentence. Circle Yes or No.

1. Look at Picture 19
   Miguel wants to help Rosa open a restaurant.

   19  (YES)   NO

2. Look at Picture 30
   Rosa wants to serve Mexican food.

   30    YES   NO

3. Look at Picture 36
   Mr. Brashov tells Katherine and Rosa about a reservation.

   36    YES   NO

4. Look at Picture 40
   Katherine helps Rosa with lunch.

   40    YES   NO

5. Look at Picture 41
   Mrs. Gilroy didn't make reservations for lunch.

   41    YES   NO

6. Look at Picture 58
   Mr. Brashov's brother Nicolae comes to visit.

   58   YES   NO

Build Your Vocabulary

Rosa's Kitchen

Read the words in the list. Find the numbers in the picture.

1. cupboards
2. counter
3. drawer
4. coffeemaker
5. sink
6. stove
7. oven
8. burners
9. pan
10. refrigerator

Complete these sentences. Use the words from the picture.

1. There is a postcard on the side of the white _____refrigerator (10)_____ .

2. Rosa cooks on the _____ behind her.

3. The stove has four _____ to cook on.

4. Rosa cooks eggs in the _____ on top of the stove.

5. Every morning Rosa uses her _____ to make coffee.

6. She keeps her dishes in the _____ above the counter.

7. She keeps her knives and forks in the _____ next to the stove.

8. Rosa washes her dishes in the kitchen _____ .

9. Her coffeemaker is on the _____ .

Picture Dictionary

Study the picture and the English word. Copy the word. Then you may write the word in your language.

1.

flowers

f l o w e r s

_ _ _ _ _ _ _

my language

2.

menu

_ _ _ _

_____

3.

Mexico

_ _ _ _ _ _

_____

4.

necklace

_ _ _ _ _ _ _ _

_____

5.

package

_ _ _ _ _ _ _

_____

6.

pillow

_ _ _ _ _ _

_____

7.

Puebla

_ _ _ _ _ _

_____

8.

surprised

_ _ _ _ _ _ _ _ _

_____

9.

worry

_ _ _ _ _

_____

Glossary

conference: meeting of many people. *There were 5,000 people at the nurses' conference.*

manage: take care of, handle. *Because she manages her money well, she can take an expensive vacation.*

reservation: a place saved in advance. *We made hotel reservations for next Saturday.*

roommate: a person who lives with someone. *She wants a roommate to help pay the rent.*

successful: do very well. *The sale was very successful. They bought everything.*

Jamal sees two friends at a party. They ask about his job. He doesn't tell the truth. When Jamal's friends come to the café, they find out the truth.

What is the truth about Jamal?

Who's in This Story?

Jamal
the café handyman

Jihan
Jamal's wife

Mohammed
a friend of Jamal's

Abdullah
a friend of Jamal's

a reporter

Katherine
the waitress

Rosa
the cook

Victor Brashov
the café owner

Jess
a regular customer

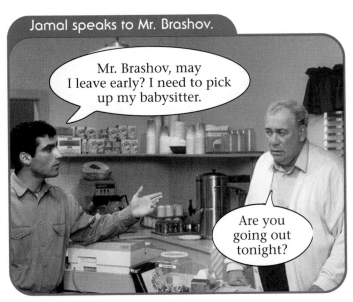

7

✓ **Check Yourself**

1. Why does Mr. Brashov wait for a phone call?
   a. He wants to order something.
   b. He wants someone from the newspaper to call.

2. Why does Jamal want to leave early?
   a. He wants to go to a party.
   b. He wants to go to a movie.

8

Later that evening at the party . . .

9

10

11

12

13

14

15

16

17

18

19

20

21

22

23

24

25

26

27

28

29

30

31

Jamal begins to act like the boss.

Katherine, bring some coffee over here. Where's Henry? He should be back from that delivery.

32

Rosa, are you working on tomorrow's special?

Excuse me?

What do you think you are do . . . ?

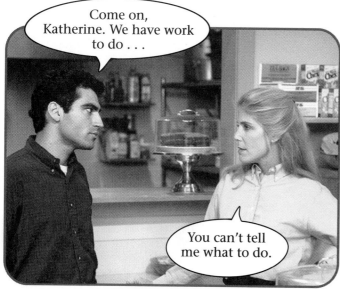

33

Come on, Katherine. We have work to do . . .

You can't tell me what to do.

34

Come into the kitchen!

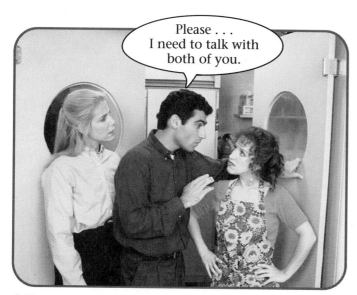

35

Please . . . I need to talk with both of you.

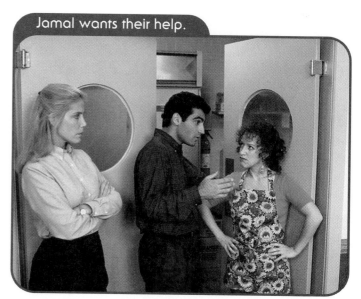

36

Jamal wants their help.

37

38

39

40

41

42

4 Who's the Boss? —— **59**

43

44

45

46

47

48

49

50

51

52

53

54

55

Jamal, isn't that the handyman's job?

Yes, it is the handyman's job. And I am the handyman.

Then who is the owner of the restaurant?

That is the owner, Mr. Victor Brashov.

56

It's nice to meet you. I'm sorry for the mix-up. It was an experiment.

An experiment? Can you tell me more about it?

57

✓ **Check Yourself**

7. Why does a reporter come to the café?
   a. to talk with the owner
   b. to fix the alarm

8. How do Abdullah and Mohammed learn Jamal is the handyman?
   a. Jamal tells them.
   b. The reporter tells them.

58

I'm sorry. I lied to you. I told you I was the owner. But . . . I am only the handyman.

59

Why didn't you tell us about your job?

I was ashamed to tell you the truth.

60

61

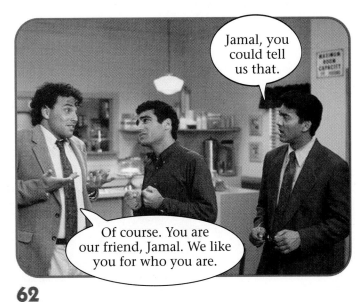

62

63

64

65

66

67

68

This is a great review. Congratulations!

69

I want to thank you all. The favor you did . . . I am happy to have good friends like you.

70

71

✓ Check Yourself

9. What does Jess read?
   a. a story about the café
   b. a story about the neighborhood

10. What does the reporter write in the newspaper?
   a. that Mr. Brashov works very hard
   b. that Mr. Brashov is a good friend to his employees

72

Tell the Story

Put the pictures and sentences in order. For each story, number 1 to 3. Then tell each story to someone.

Jamal's Story

___ a.

Jamal tells the truth to his friends.

__1__ b.

Jamal sees his friends at a party.

___ c.

Jamal acts like the boss.

Reporter's Story

___ a.

Mr. Brashov meets the reporter.

___ b.

Jess reads the Crossroads Café review.

___ c.

Mr. Brashov tells Jess about the *Restaurant News*.

Search

Unscramble the word. Complete the sentence.

1. The alarm is near the _d_ _o_ _o_ _r_ in the café. (o d r o)

2. There is a big __ __ __ __ __ of food at the party. (a p t l e)

3. Mohammed and Abdullah sit at the __ __ __ __ __. (a t e b l)

4. Jamal works with the __ __ __ __ __. (r w i s e)

5. Jamal tells a __ __ __ to his friends. (i l e)

6. The reporter writes for the __ __ __ __ __ __ __ __ __. (p n a s r e w e p)

Now find each word below. When you find a word, circle it.

A	Z	G	F	L	W	I	R	E	S
V	A	T	E	I	D	G	L	C	D
P	L	A	T	E	Q	K	M	B	D
Y	H	B	H	I	J	F	D	N	O
X	I	L	O	P	R	L	E	W	O
B	N	E	W	S	P	A	P	E	R
C	J	K	T	U	S	M	S	U	Q

Build Your Vocabulary

A Party

Read the words in the list. Find the numbers in the picture.

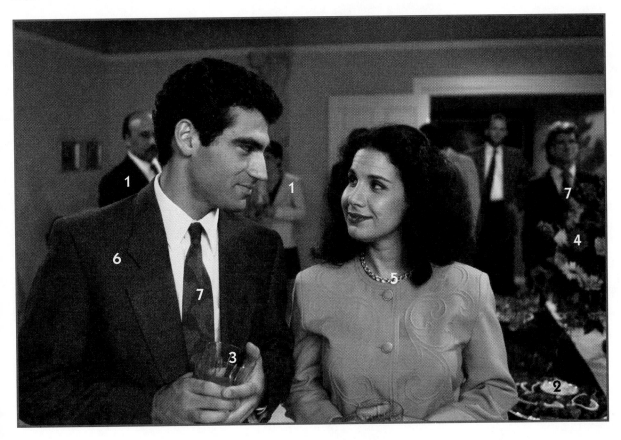

1. guests
2. food
3. glass
4. flowers
5. necklace
6. suit
7. ties

Complete the sentences. Use the words from the picture.

1. Jamal is wearing a new _____suit (6)_____.

2. Jamal has a _____ in his hand.

3. Many _____ come to the party.

4. The men are wearing _____ around their necks.

5. There are beautiful _____ on the table.

6. Jihan is wearing a pretty _____ around her neck.

7. There is a plate of _____ on the table.

Picture Dictionary

Study the picture and the English word. Copy the word. Then you may write the word in your language.

1.

alarm

a l a r m

_ _ _ _ _ _ _ _ _ _ _ _

my language

2.

ashamed

_ _ _ _ _ _ _

_ _ _ _ _ _ _ _ _ _ _ _

3.

Cairo

_ _ _ _ _

_ _ _ _ _ _ _ _ _ _ _ _

4.

Egypt

_ _ _ _ _

_ _ _ _ _ _ _ _ _ _ _ _

5.

list

_ _ _ _

_ _ _ _ _ _ _ _ _ _ _ _

6.

newspaper

_ _ _ _ _ _ _ _ _

_ _ _ _ _ _ _ _ _ _ _ _

7.

proud

_ _ _ _ _ .

_ _ _ _ _ _ _ _ _ _ _ _

8.

reporter

_ _ _ _ _ _ _ _

_ _ _ _ _ _ _ _ _ _ _ _

Glossary

apologize: To say you are sorry for doing or saying something wrong. *Marisa wants to apologize to her father for breaking the window.*

boss: A person in charge of others. *When the secretary is going to be late for work, he calls his boss.*

laid off: To lose a job even if you did nothing wrong. *The worker was laid off because there was no money to pay her.*

lie: Something that is not true. *Don't lie to me. You said you went to school, but you didn't.*

pretend: to act in a make believe or false way. *The man likes to pretend he is rich.*

truth: Something that is correct or true. *Dad, the truth is I took your car without asking. I'm sorry.*

5 Lost and Found

Jess and Carol are at home. A policeman is asking them questions. They are answering his questions.

What information does the policeman want?

Who's in This Story?

Jess
a regular customer
at the café

Carol
Jess's wife

a salesman

Katherine
the waitress

David
Katherine's son

Jamal
the handyman

Rosa
the cook

Henry
the busboy and
delivery person

Victor Brashov
the café owner

1

2

3

4

5

6

The policeman leaves and Carol and Jess are alone.

Oh, no. Not the plane?

Yeah.

I'm sorry, Jess.

7

Tomorrow, I'm going to call some security companies.

Jess, nobody was hurt.

This time we are O.K. But what about next time?

8

I'm not going to live in a house with bars and steel doors.

Well, I'm not going to live like this.

9

✓ **Check Yourself**

1. What happened to Jess's plane?
   a. Someone took it.
   b. Someone broke it.

2. Who is Jess going to call?
   a. some security companies
   b. his neighbors

10

A few days later at Crossroads Café . . .

Rosa, can you come here? I need your help.

All right.

Yes, I'm David's mother. David isn't at school? I had no idea.

11

12

13

14

15

16

17

18

19

20

21

22

23

24

25

Why don't you leave me alone?

Because I'm your mother.

26

I don't need a mother.

✓ **Check Yourself**

3. Why does Mr. Brashov need Rosa's help?

   a. because Katherine is on the phone

   b. because Katherine is sick

4. What did the school counselor tell Katherine?

   a. that David got hurt at school

   b. that David didn't go to school

27

That night Jess and Carol meet with a salesman.

28

Our company provides full security.

29

Put bars on your windows. Nobody will break in.

Like a jail.

30

31

32

33

34

35

36

37

38

39

40

41

42

43

44

45

46

47

48

49

50

51

52

53

54

✓ **Check Yourself**

7. Why doesn't David build things with his father anymore?
   a. His father isn't good at building things.
   b. His father doesn't live with him.

8. When Jess's father left home, what did he leave for Jess?
   a. a note and some money
   b. a note and an airplane

The next night, Jamal helps Carol and Jess install a burglar alarm.

What does it say next?

Place the green wire into the blue wire which is to the right of the red wire.

55

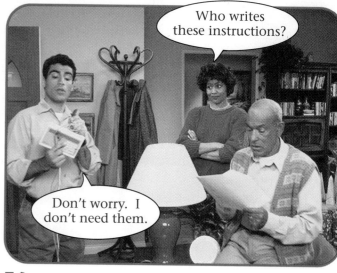

Who writes these instructions?

Don't worry. I don't need them.

56

All right. The green goes here. Then the blue. Then the red. That's what the instructions were trying to say.

57

All right. Carol, go outside and close the door. I'll set the alarm.

O.K.

Cover your ears when you come in. It will be loud. Go ahead Jess.

58

O.K., Carol. Come back in.

59

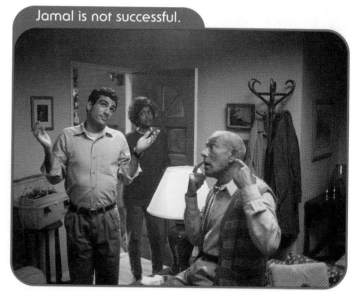

Jamal is not successful.

60

80   Crossroads Café   Photo Stories A

61

62

63

64

65

66

The next day at Crossroads Café . . .

Katherine, what are you looking for?

David. He's late.

Some kids are never on time.

67

More coffee, Jess?

No, thank you.

68

Ah, David. Come in.

69

Where were you?

At the woodshop at school.

70

A friend of mine has an old model airplane that needs some work.

71

✓ **Check Yourself**

9. What do Jess and Carol try to do to make their house safe?

   a. put bars on their windows

   b. install an alarm system

10. Why does Carol invite people from the neighborhood to her house?

    a. to play cards

    b. to fight crime

72

Tell the Story

Put the pictures and sentences in order. For each story, number 1 to 3. Then tell each story to someone.

Jess and Carol's Story

____ a.

Carol invites people from the neighborhood to fight against crime.

1 b.

Someone broke into Jess and Carol's house.

____ c.

Jamal tries to install an alarm for Jess and Carol.

Katherine and David's Story

____ a.

David uses Jamal's tools.

____ b.

David says he might work on Jess's plane.

____ c.

Jess and David talk about their fathers.

Search

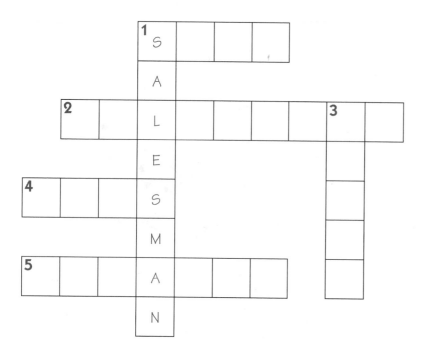

Complete the sentences. Then finish the puzzle above.

Across

1. Jess locks his door in order to feel _____.

2. The _____ asked Jess and Carol questions.

4. Carol doesn't want _____ on her windows.

5. When people _____ to your house, you should report missing things to the police.

Down

1. Jess asked the company to send a _____salesman_____ to his house.

3. Jess bought an _____ and asked Jamal to install it.

Build Your Vocabulary

Jamal's Workbench

Read the words in the list. Find the numbers in the picture.

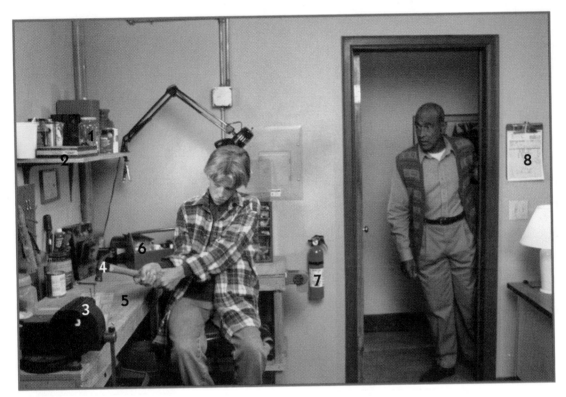

1. jar
2. shelf
3. vise
4. hammer
5. workbench
6. toolbox
7. fire extinguisher
8. clipboard

Complete the sentences. Use the words from the picture.

1. David is sitting at Jamal's _____workbench (5)_____.

2. David is using a _____ to make something.

3. A _____ is above the workbench.

4. There is a glass _____ with bolts on the shelf.

5. There is a red _____ on the wall behind David.

6. A _____ is hanging on the wall next to the door.

7. A metal _____ is at the end of the workbench.

8. The tools are in the _____ next to David.

Picture Dictionary

Study the picture and the English word. Copy the word. Then you may write the word in your language.

1.

alarm

a l a r m

_____
my language

2.

(steel) bars

— — — —

3.

hammer

— — — — — —

4.

keys

— — — —

5.

nails

— — — — —

6.

plane

— — — — —

7.

tools

— — — — —

8.

wires

— — — — —

9.

wood

— — — —

Glossary

break in: to enter without permission. *The gang is planning to break in to the school and steal computers.*

counselor: a person who gives advice. *Before they get a divorce they should see a counselor.*

kids: children. *She needs someone to take care of her kids.*

neighbor: a person who lives near. *I have a cup of coffee with my neighbor every morning.*

playground: a place where children play. *Most elementary schools have a playground.*

security company: a business that sells things to make people feel safe. *The alarm in this house is hooked up to a security company.*

6 Time Is Money

Mr. Brashov has a lot of paperwork. He doesn't like paperwork. A friend of Jess's comes to help him.

How does Jess's friend change things at the café?

Who's in This Story?

Victor Brashov
the café owner

Jess Washington
a regular customer

Emery Bradford
a friend of Jess's son

Rosa
the cook and a
night school student

Rosa's teacher

Armando
Rosa's classmate

Katherine
the waitress

Henry
the busboy and
delivery person

Jamal
the handyman

7

8

9

10

11

12

13

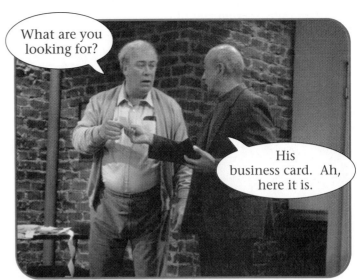

14

✓ **Check Yourself**

1. Mr. Brashov says
   a. he likes paperwork
   b. he doesn't like paperwork

2. Jess gives Mr. Brashov a friend's business card because
   a. his friend wants a job
   b. his friend can help Mr. Brashov

15

16

17

18

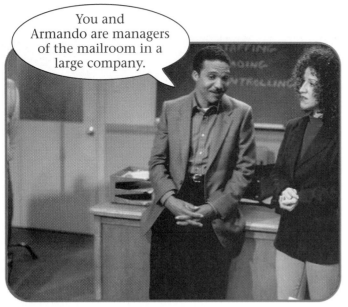

19

You and Armando are managers of the mailroom in a large company.

20

Your employees have to pack these boxes before the post office closes.

21

Armando's team goes to work.

That's right. Take your time.

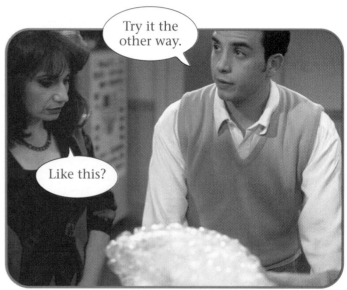

22

Try it the other way.

Like this?

23

Armando's team finishes.

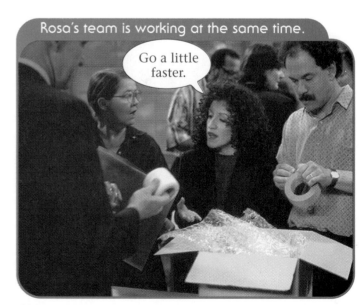

24

Rosa's team is working at the same time.

Go a little faster.

25

26

27

28

29

30

A few days later, Mr. Bradford comes to help.

31

Divide your bills into groups—like rent, supplies, utilities.

But there are so many bills. I need to know when to pay.

32

Mr. Bradford stops to watch Katherine.

That's interesting

What is?

33

Mr. Bradford tells Mr. Brashov that Katherine wastes time when she puts her pencil behind her ear.

34

Time is money.

35

✓ **Check Yourself**

5. Mr. Bradford helps Mr. Brashov
   a. organize his bills
   b. pay his bills

6. Mr. Bradford tells Mr. Brashov that time is like
   a. bills
   b. money

36

A few days later at Crossroads Café, Mr. Bradford watches Mr. Brashov talk about a delivery.

Did I say 25 minutes? I mean we will be there in 20 minutes.

37

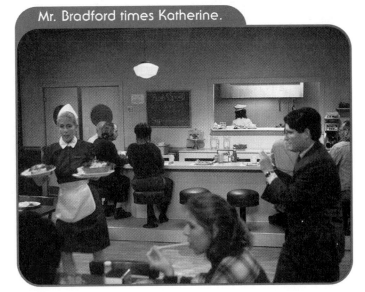

Mr. Bradford times Katherine.

38

Look how fast your people are working. Each one wants to win the contest.

I know this contest is a good idea, but I'm not sure I can pay the $100 prize.

39

One week later at Crossroads Café . . .

Where is my order?

I'm cooking it.

Hurry. I am not going to lose this contest because of you.

40

Where are you going?

To Bidwell's Hardware Store for a filter for the air conditioner.

41

Why don't you go to Joe's Hardware?

Filters are cheaper at Bidwell's.

42

43

How do you know?

I called the stores. Mr. Bradford said we should compare prices.

44

Good work, Jamal.

45

46

So, Victor are you ready to name the winner of your contest?

Mr. Bradford's contest. Not mine.

Late afternoon the next day at Crossroads Café . . .

The café is more efficient now. It is moving in the right direction.

47

And now, the winner of the contest . . .

48

49

50

51

52

53

54

55

You did something very special for this restaurant. Now, you can help another business.

56

But, Mr. Brashov, there is still much to do here.

And we will do it.

57

But Mr. Brashov.

Thank you and good-bye.

58

That is much better

59

Late the next day at Crossroads Café . . .

Well, Victor, you have lots of paperwork again.

I have lots of paperwork, but now I am more organized.

60

✓ **Check Yourself**

9. Mr. Brashov gives the prize to
   a. Emery
   b. Rosa

10. Mr. Brashov still has paperwork, but now
    a. there is more of it
    b. it is more organized

Tell the Story

Match the picture with the sentence. Then tell the story to someone.

_____ 1.

_____ 2.

_____ 3.

_____ 4.

a. Jess gives Emery's business card to Mr. Brashov.

b. Mr. Brashov tells Emery good-bye.

c. Mr. Brashov has a lot of paperwork.

d. Emery helps Mr. Brashov.

Search

Look at the picture. Read the sentence. Circle Yes or No.

1. Look at picture 3

   Mr. Brashov has trouble with the calculator.

   3  (YES) NO

2. Look at picture 28

   Rosa feels good about her management class.

   28  YES NO

3. Look at picture 34

   Mr. Bradford wants Katherine to waste time.

   34  YES NO

4. Look at picture 40

   Katherine wants to win the contest.

   40  YES NO

5. Look at picture 42

   Mr. Bradford wants Jamal to save money.

   42  YES NO

6. Look at picture 50

   Katherine thinks everyone should win the prize.

   50  YES NO

Answer Key: *Search:* 1. yes; 2. no, She feels bad about her management class; 3. no, Mr. Bradford wants Katherine to save time; 4. yes; 5. yes; 6. no, Rosa thinks everyone should win the prize.

Build Your Vocabulary

Wrapping Packages

Read the words in the list. Find the numbers in the picture.

1. scissors
2. tape
3. box
4. bubble wrap
5. wrapping paper
6. string

Complete the sentences. Use the words from the picture.

1. Before you put the plates in the box, put _____bubble wrap (4)_____ around them.

2. Use _____ to cut pieces of tape.

3. Use the _____ to close the box.

4. After you close the box with tape, put _____ around the box.

5. Finally put _____ around the box and tie it.

6. Now you can mail the _____.

Picture Dictionary

Study the picture and the English word. Copy the word. Then you may write the word in your language.

1.

bill

b i l l

2.

box

___

3.

business card

_ _ _ _ _ _

4.

calculator

_ _ _ _ _ _

5.

paperwork

_ _ _ _ _ _

6.

prize

_ _ _ _

Glossary

air conditioner: a machine that makes the air cool. *It is too warm in here. Turn up the air conditioner.*

contest: competition. *A soccer game is a contest between two teams.*

divide: separate. *There are six of us. Divide the pie into six pieces.*

efficient: work well and quickly. *Her boss promoted her because she is very efficient.*

organize: to put in order. *Please organize these dishes. Put the plates on one shelf, and the cups and glasses on another shelf.*

Fish Out of Water

Mr. Brashov's brother Nicolae comes to visit. He learns many things about the café and the United States. He makes a decision about his life.

What is Nicolae's decision?

Who's in This Story?

Nicolae Brashov
Mr. Brashov's brother

Victor Brashov
the café owner

a Romanian band

a man from the mall

Rosa
the cook

Katherine
the waitress

Jamal
the handyman

Jess
a regular customer

Henry
the busboy and
delivery person

1

One morning at the café . . .

2

Can I put this banner up now?

Yes, but hurry. They'll be here soon.

3

WELCOME TO Crossroads C

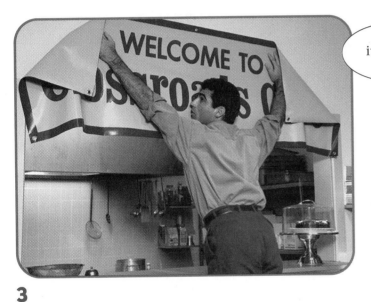

4

Mr. Brashov comes in the café with his brother, Nicolae.

Victor, it is like a palace.

This is Crossroads Café. And this is Katherine, Rosa, Jamal, Henry . . . and Jess.

5

Jess Washington.

Meet Crossroads Café's best customer.

6

My friends, this is my brother and new business partner, Nicolae Brashov.

Hello, Mr. Brashov.

Please, please. Call me Nicolae.

7 "So, what do you think?" "Everything is just like you said."

✓ **Check Yourself**

1. Who is Nicolae?
   a. a customer
   b. Mr. Brashov's brother

2. What does Nicolae think of the café?
   a. He likes it.
   b. He doesn't like it.

8

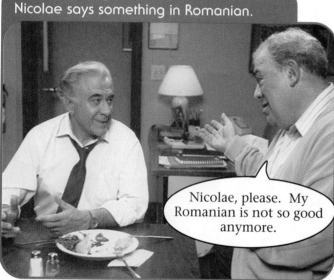

9 Later that night Nicolae and Victor talk. Nicolae says something in Romanian.

"Nicolae, please. My Romanian is not so good anymore."

10 "You don't remember your own language." "With Eva gone, there is no one to talk to."

11 Mr. Brashov sneezes.

"Bless you."

12 "I don't feel well. I think I'm getting sick." "You need a bowl of Mama's stew."

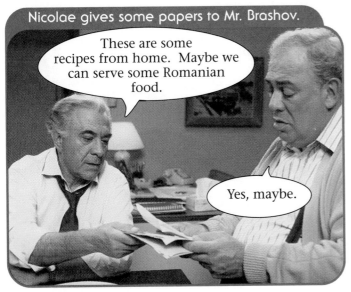

Nicolae gives some papers to Mr. Brashov.

These are some recipes from home. Maybe we can serve some Romanian food.

Yes, maybe.

13

I'm sorry, Victor. It was a stupid idea.

No, not at all . . .

14

Victor, you should get some rest.

You're right. Let's go home.

15

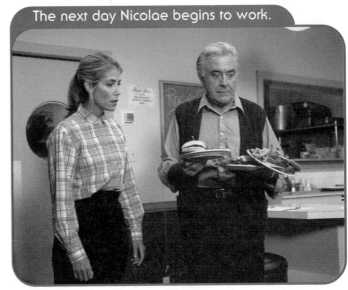

The next day Nicolae begins to work.

16

17

This time Nicolae does a better job.

18

7   Fish Out of Water   **107**

19

20

21

22

23

24

25

Excuse me, is it O.K. if I make a few changes?

Sure.

26

He makes changes in the supply list.

27

He makes changes in the café.

So, how is Mr. Brashov?

The patient is better. He is coming in tomorrow.

28

Oh, that's wonderful.

Yes, I need to make sure that everything is ready.

29

✓ **Check Yourself**

3. What does Nicolae do at the café?
   a. He rides his bike.
   b. He serves food to the customers.

4. Why is Nicolae in charge of the café?
   a. Mr. Brashov goes on a trip.
   b. Mr. Brashov is sick.

30

The next morning at the café . . .

31

I can't wait for Victor to see this. It will make him feel like he is at home in Romania.

32

Mr. Brashov comes into the café.

Ah, Victor, welcome back. Isn't this wonderful?

33

Stop the music! This is a restaurant, not a cheap Romanian cabaret.

34

Nicolae apologizes in Romanian.

I'm sorry.

35

Victor, I don't understand. I was trying to make this place more like home.

36

My home is here . . . in this country.

If you live here, does it change who you are?

I am the same person I always was.

No, you are not. You are ashamed of where you come from . . . our customs . . . our language . . .

37

I don't want to talk about this anymore.

What happened to you, Victor? I don't want it to happen to me!

38

Mr. Brashov rips the poster of Romania off the wall.

39

✓ **Check Yourself**

5. How does Mr. Brashov feel when he comes back to work?
   a. sad
   b. angry

6. Why does Mr. Brashov get upset with Nicolae?
   a. He doesn't like the changes in the café.
   b. He wants Nicolae to work more.

40

Nicolae leaves the café and goes to a shopping mall.

41

The people make Nicolae uncomfortable.

42

Nicolae drops his wallet.

43

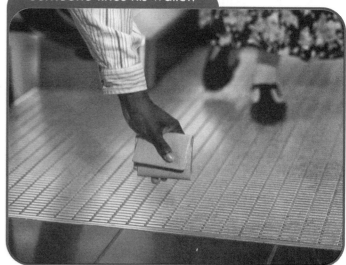

Someone finds his wallet.

44

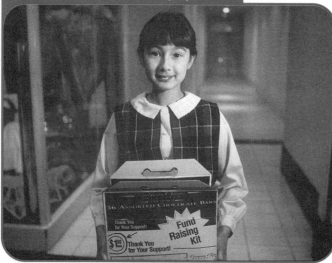

A girl offers Nicolae candy. He doesn't know he has to pay.

45

46

A policeman stops Nicolae.

Did you pay for that candy? Let's see some identification.

47

The policeman frightens Nicolae.

48

Nicolae thinks about when he was a boy in Romania.

49

He hears Romanian music.

50

He stands at a door and listens.

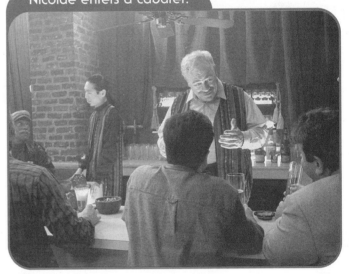

51

Nicolae enters a cabaret.

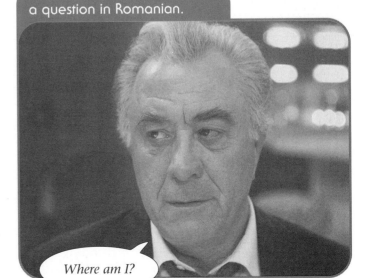

52

A Romanian invites Nicolae to sit down.

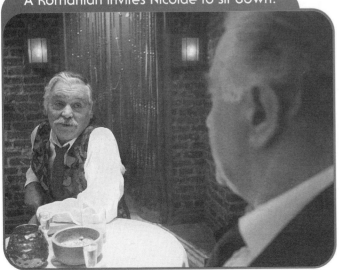

53

Nicolae feels lost. He asks a question in Romanian.

Where am I?

54

The man answers in Romanian.

You are home.

55

Nicolae knows what he has to do.

56

Another day at Crossroads Café.

Are you all right, Mr. Brashov?

Yes, I'm fine . . . No, I'm not fine.

57

Nicolae doesn't want to stay. He's going home. I wanted the United States to be his home.

Mr. Brashov, I have lived here for five years. It never feels like home.

58

I thought you were happy here.

I am. But, sometimes I miss my family, my friends, and my language.

59

What's in the bag, Mr. Brashov?

Everyone looks at the bag.

Something Nicolae gave me before he left.

60

61

It's beautiful.

Nicolae said it was to remember him.

62

A man comes into the café.

Hi. Is Nicholas Brashov here?

No. Nicolae is not here. I am Victor Brashov, his brother.

63

I found his wallet at the shopping mall. Your address was on a piece of paper in the wallet. So, I came to return it.

64

Thank you. You are very kind. Would you like to have something to eat?

No, thanks, I need to get back to work.

Thank you. Goodbye.

65

Brashov looks at the things in the wallet.

And poor Nicolae thought someone stole his wallet. Money . . . identification . . . cards . . . pictures . . .

66

What is it, Mr. Brashov?

An old picture.

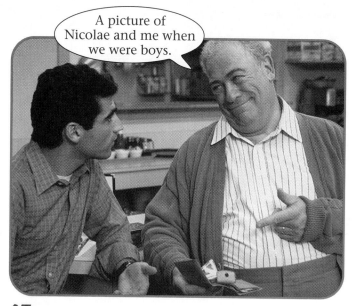

67 A picture of Nicolae and me when we were boys.

68 Mr. Brashov thinks about when Nicolae will leave.

69 Mr. Brashov makes a telephone call to the airport.

Did flight #1745 leave yet? Good. Can you page Nicolae Brashov for me, please?

70 Hello, Nicolae? No, everything is O.K. Someone found your wallet. Yes, I know you need to go.

71 I want to visit you soon. We can go for a bicycle ride . . . like the old days.

72

✓ **Check Yourself**

9. What does Nicolae do?

   a. He stays in the United States.

   b. He goes back to Romania.

10. Why does the man come to the café?

   a. to return a wallet

   b. to get something to eat

Tell the Story

Put the pictures and sentences in order. Number 1 to 6. Then tell the story to someone.

____ a.

Mr. Brashov looks sadly
at a picture.

__1__ b.

Mr. Brashov shows Nicolae
the café.

____ c.

When Mr. Brashov sees the
band, he becomes angry.

____ d.

Nicolae learns about the café.

____ e.

Nicolae thinks about Romania.

____ f.

Mr. Brashov calls the airport
to say goodbye.

Search

Unscramble the word. Complete the sentence.

1. The _____banner_____ reads, "Welcome to Crossroads Café." (n a b e r n)

2. The woman is sad because she can't find her _____. (t w a l e l)

3. The colors of the United States _____ are red, white and blue. (g l a f)

4. The customer asks the chef for the _____ for chocolate cake. (e c p r i e)

5. The woman put her gifts in a _____ _____.
   (n i s p h o p g   g b a)

6. Henry plays music in a _____. (d n a b)

7. There is a large _____ on the wall. (e p o t r s)

8. The _____ _____ plays a nice song. (s i m u c   x b o)

Now find each word below. When you find a word, circle it.

```
B  A  N  N  E  R  H  A  P  E  F
P  D  H  O  X  C  B  K  Q  Z  L
O  I  Y  A  B  L  A  O  J  C  A
S  H  O  P  P  I  N  G  B  A  G
T  D  L  B  G  M  D  F  P  G  R
E  M  U  S  I  C  B  O  X  H  I
R  E  C  I  P  E  F  G  V  W  S
N  M  E  K  F  W  A  L  L  E  T
```

Build Your Vocabulary

Romanian Decorations

Read the words in the list. Find the numbers in the picture.

1. salami
2. flag
3. baskets
4. garlic
5. pitchers
6. tray
7. cheese
8. frying pan

Complete the sentences. Use the words from the picture.

1. There are three _____ pitchers (5) _____. Two are filled with water.

2. A small Romanian _____ is on the counter.

3. There is an empty _____ under the window.

4. _____ is a kind of meat. It is hanging near the window.

5. Many _____ are hanging above the window.

6. Rosa hangs her large _____ on the wall in the kitchen.

7. The cook puts a lot of _____ in the spaghetti sauce.

8. Large round _____ balls are hanging above the window.

Picture Dictionary

Study the picture and the English word. Copy the word. Then you may write the word in your language.

1.

band

b a n d

_____
my language

2.

banner

_ _ _ _ _ _
_____

3.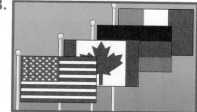

flags

_ _ _ _ _
_____

4.

music box

_ _ _ _ _ _ _ _
_____

5.

picture

_ _ _ _ _ _ _
_____

6.

poster

_ _ _ _ _ _
_____

7.

shopping bag

_ _ _ _ _ _ _ _ _ _ _
_____

8.

wallet

_ _ _ _ _ _
_____

Glossary

ashamed: feeling guilty and sad about something wrong. *He feels ashamed because he failed his driver's test.*

cabaret: a restaurant which offers drinks and a singing and dancing show. *Everyone had a good time at the cabaret.*

flu: a sickness with a fever, chills, headache, and body aches. *Many people are sick with the flu during the winter.*

mall: an enclosed public area with many stores and eating places. *Some teenagers like to spend time at the mall.*

partner: a person that shares something with another. *My partner at school helped me write a report.*

recipe: a set of directions to make something to eat. *The cook has a recipe for every meal he makes.*

8 Family Matters

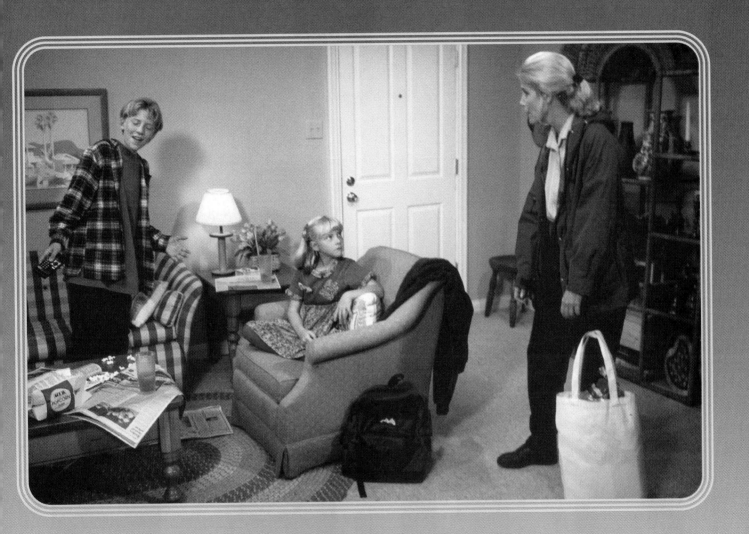

Katherine is very tired. The workers at
the café worry about her. Katherine worries
about her son. Rosa discovers the problem.
She helps Katherine.

Why is Katherine tired?

Who's in This Story?

Katherine
the café waitress
a single mother
of two

David
Katherine's
teenage son

Suzanne
Katherine's
8-year-old
daughter

Henry
the busboy and
delivery person
a high school student

Sara
a high school
student in Henry's
Social Studies class

Victor Brashov
the café owner

Rosa
the cook

Jess
a regular customer

Jamal
the handyman

1

2

3

4

5

6

7

8

9

10

11

12

13

14

15

16

17

18

19

20

21

22

23

24

25

26

27

28

29

30

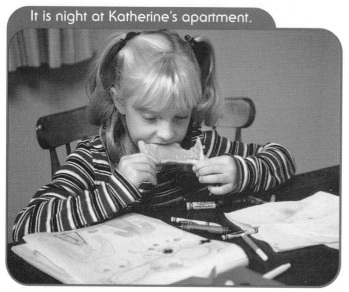

It is night at Katherine's apartment.

31

Hi, Suzanne. I'm Rosa. Do you remember me? I work with your mom.

Sure. Come on in.

32

Is your mom here?

No. She isn't home from work yet.

33

But the café closed hours ago.

Not the café. Her other job.

A second job?

34

What are you drawing?

A picture of me and David.

35

May I see it?

Sure.

36

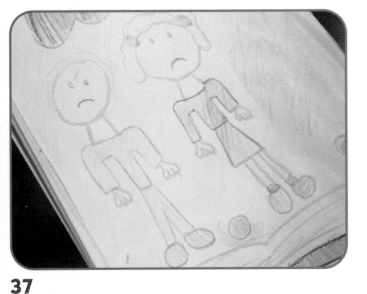

37

✓ **Check Yourself**

5. How does Rosa find out about Katherine's second job?
   a. Katherine tells her.
   b. Suzanne tells her.

6. What does Suzanne draw a picture of?
   a. two happy children
   b. two unhappy children

38

Katherine returns home.

Rosa! What are you doing here?

I went to the sale at the department store.

39

I bought you these nylons.

Thanks, but I . . . uh . . . I really don't need them.

40

So what are you really doing here?

I was worried about you.

41

Worried? Why? I am just a little tired.

I know.

42

43

44

45

46

47

48

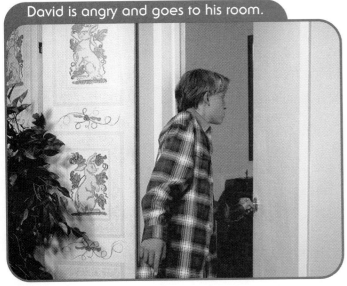

David is angry and goes to his room.

49

50

The next day at Crossroads Café . . .

Are you all right.

No. Last night David locked himself in his room. This morning he wouldn't talk to me.

51

May I use the phone to check on my kids?

Of course. Is something wrong?

I'm not sure.

52

Henry comes to work.

Henry! Are you all right?

No. Sara won't talk to me.

53

I leave messages, but she won't call back.

54

55 Katherine hangs up the phone.

I have to leave, Mr. Brashov. David and Suzanne are not home from school.

56

Did you call the school?

Yes. They left an hour ago.

57

Where could they be?

I don't know. David is angry because of the divorce.

58

David is not doing well in school. I thought a computer would help. I wanted to buy him a computer for his birthday.

So that's why you asked me about computers.

59

Computers are expensive. I had to take another job in the evenings.

60

✓ Check Yourself

7. Why is David unhappy?
   a. because his mother is never home
   b. because Rosa came to visit

8. Why did Katherine take a second job?
   a. to buy clothes for Suzanne
   b. to buy a computer for David

61

My children need me. Now it may be too late. I think they ran away.

No we didn't, Mom.

62

What are you doing here?

I wanted to give Mr. Washington back his airplane.

63

Also, I'm sorry about last night.

64

Would you like to celebrate your birthday early? We can go to the lake for the weekend . . . just the three of us.

Great. Can we go fishing?

65

Katherine and her children leave the café. Sara enters the café.

May I help you?

Yes. Is Henry here?

66

Sara? What are you doing here?

You left a message.

67

68

69

70

71

✓ Check Yourself

9. Why does Katherine quit her second job?
   a. Her children need her.
   b. She doesn't like it.

10. Why does Katherine want to go to the lake?
    a. She wants to spend time with her children.
    b. She wants a vacation from work.

72

Tell the Story

Put the pictures and sentences in order. Number 1 to 5. Then tell the story to someone.

 a.

Katherine sees her daughter's drawing.

___ b.

Katherine decides time with her children is important.

<u>1</u> c.

Katherine wants to buy a computer for David.

___ d.

Rosa goes to Katherine's apartment.

___ e.

Suzanne tells Rosa about Katherine's second job.

Search

Look at the picture. Read the sentence. Circle Yes or No.

1. **Look at Picture 10**
   Jamal says computers are cheap.

   10    YES   (NO)

2. **Look at Picture 13**
   David and Suzanne want to watch the same program.

   13    YES   NO

3. **Look at Picture 25**
   Katherine makes the customer happy.

   25    YES   NO

4. **Look at Picture 29**
   Rosa teaches Henry to draw.

   29    YES   NO

5. **Look at Picture 68**
   Henry asks Sara to the dance.

   68    YES   NO

Build Your Vocabulary

Katherine's Home

Read the words in the list. Find the numbers in the pictures.

The Living Room

1. sofa
2. TV remote control
3. chair
4. coffee table
5. homework
6. television

The Dining Room Table

7. table
8. drawing
9. crayons

Complete the sentences. Use the words from the pictures.

1. David and Suzanne are fighting over the ___TV remote control (2)___.

2. David is sitting in a _____.

3. Suzanne is sitting on a green and white _____.

4. We can see the back of the _____.

5. A _____ is between the sofa and the television.

6. David's _____ is on the coffee table.

7. Suzanne is looking at a _____ and eating.

8. She made the drawing with _____.

9. There are flowers on the _____.

Picture Dictionary

Study the picture and the English word. Copy the word. Then you may write the word in your language.

1.

airplane

a i r p l a n e

_____

my language

2.

balloon

_____

_____

3.

cartoon

_____

_____

4.

computer

_____

_____

5.

dance

_____

_____

6.

drawing

_____

_____

7.

homework

_____

_____

8.

tired

_____

_____

9.

tuxedo

_____

_____

Glossary

babysit: take care of children when their parents are not home. *High school students babysit to earn money.*

check on: look at to see if O.K. *Please check on the food. I put it in the oven an hour ago; it should be ready.*

date: a meeting with someone for fun. *He made a date with me for dinner.*

divorce: the end of a marriage. *Her parents are divorced and she lives with her mother.*

run away: leave home. *Sometimes children are unhappy with their parents and run away.*

Rush to Judgment

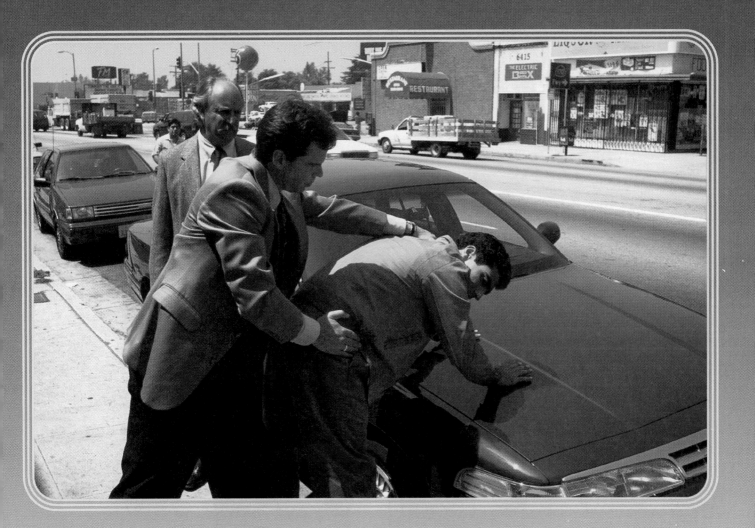

The police are looking for a burglar.
The burglar looks like Jamal. The police
see Jamal on the street. They ask him
many questions.

What happens to Jamal?

Who's in This Story?

Jamal
the café handyman

Detective Anderson
a police officer

Detective Benton
a police officer

Henry
the busboy and
delivery person

Grandma Chang
Henry's
grandmother

Grandpa Chang
Henry's
grandfather

Mrs. Chang
Henry's mother

Officer Kang
a police officer

Officer Seltzer
a police officer

Victor Brashov
the café owner

Katherine
the waitress

Jess
a regular customer

Rosa
the cook

1

2

3

4

5

6

7

8

9

10

11

✔ **Check Yourself**

1. Who does Mr. Brashov welcome to the neighborhood?

   a. Jess's friends

   b. police officers

2. Why are Grandpa and Grandma Chang in the café?

   a. Henry is giving them directions.

   b. They want something to eat.

12

13

14

15

16

17

18

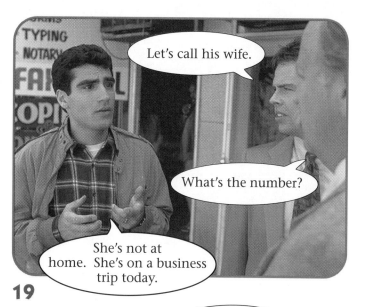

19

Let's call his wife.

What's the number?

She's not at home. She's on a business trip today.

The police officer pushes Jamal against the car.

I did nothing wrong!

He's clean.

20

Put your hands behind your back.

Am I under arrest?

If your story is true, you can leave.

21

✓ Check Yourself

3. Why do the police talk to Jamal?
   a. They help him with his tools.
   b. They think he did something wrong.

4. What do the police tell Jamal to do?
   a. to put his hands up
   b. to put his hands behind his back

22

Mr. Brashov tries to fix the coffee machine.

This is hopeless. Where is Jamal?

I don't know.

23

Ah, Jamal. Finally . . . slow down. I can't understand you. What? I'll get there as soon as I can.

24

25

26

27

28

29

30

Jamal tells his story again.

I told you, I was home last night.

31

✓ **Check Yourself**

5. Where do the police take Jamal?
   a. to the police station
   b. to Crossroads Café

6. Why do the police think Jamal is the burglar?
   a. Jamal looks like the burglar.
   b. He was carrying stolen things.

32

The Changs ask for help.

33

Henry is worried about his grandparents.

Yes, O.K. I'll wait.

34

Come on kid. I need to use the phone.

35

Mr. Brashov enters the police station.

I'm here to see Jamal Al-Jibali.

Take a seat.

36

A little later, Mr. Brashov asks again.

Can I see Jamal Al-Jibali now? I am his employer.

We're asking him some questions. He's a possible suspect.

37

At the café, Henry finally hangs up the phone.

You are making a lot of calls.

What's going on?

My grandparents are missing. This is all my fault.

38

You were helping them. I'm sure you'll find them.

39

I'm going to try to find them on my bike.

Can I drive you?

40

Well, I . . .

Come on, let's go!

Henry, don't worry. I'm sure you'll find them.

41

Where are they? They could be anywhere . . . lost . . . scared . . . maybe even hurt.

42

43

Mr. Brashov sees Detective Benton.

I know you.

The restaurant with the coffee cake. Why are you here?

44

One of my employees is here.

Is it Jamal Al-Jibali?

45

Yes. What is happening?

He looks like a burglary suspect.

46

Do you know this man?

Yes. He owns Crossroads Café.

47

Didn't the suspect say he works there?

48

49

50

51

52

53

54

55

56

Mr. Brashov enters the interrogation room.

57

58

59

60

61

62

63

64

65

66

A police officer comes to the door of the café.

I'm looking for Henry Chang.

67

Grandma, Grandpa. I'm glad you're both O.K.

68

How did you understand them?

When I was a kid I went to Chinese language school. They said you worked around here.

69

My grandparents want to thank this kind gentleman.

70

Come on. I'll give you a ride home.

71

✔ **Check Yourself**

9. What do the police tell Jamal?
   a. that he can leave the police station
   b. that he is the burglar

10. Who finds Grandma and Grandpa Chang?
    a. Henry
    b. a police officer

72

Tell the Story

Put the pictures and sentences in order. For each story, number 1 to 3. Then tell each story to someone.

Jamal's Story

____ a.

Jamal leaves the police station.

 b.

The police talk to Jamal on the street.

____ c.

The police ask Jamal many questions at the police station.

The Changs' Story

____ a.

The Changs come back to the café.

____ b.

The Changs are lost and ask for help.

____ c.

Henry tells Mr. Brashov about his grandparents.

Search

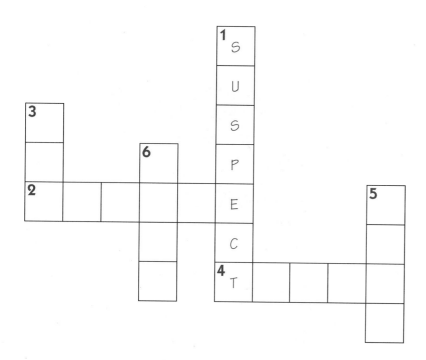

Complete the sentences. Then finish the puzzle above.

Across

2. The _____ take Jamal to the police station.

4. Jamal drops his _____ on the street.

Down

1. There was a burglary and Jamal is a _____ suspect _____.

3. The Changs look at their _____.

5. The Changs can't find the bus stop. They are _____.

6. Jamal's baby was _____.

Build Your Vocabulary

A Police Station

Read the words in the list. Find the numbers in the picture.

1. detectives
2. computer
3. badges
4. folder
5. holster
6. police officer
7. uniform
8. desk
9. pay phone

Complete the sentences. Use the words from the picture.

1. One ___police officer (6)___ in the office is wearing a uniform.

2. One policeman is wearing a blue _____.

3. There are two _____ in the room. They don't wear police uniforms.

4. Officer Seltzer and Detective Benton are wearing silver _____ for identification.

5. The police officer has a gun in the _____.

6. The detective uses a _____ to get information.

7. The detective is sitting on the _____.

8. The detective is holding a _____ in his hand.

9. There is a _____ on the wall near the map.

Picture Dictionary

Study the picture and the English word. Copy the word. Then you may write the word in your language.

1.

build

b̲ u̲ i̲ l̲ d̲

_____
my language

2.

small build

_ _ _ _ _   _ _ _ _ _

_____

3.

medium build

_ _ _ _ _ _   _ _ _ _ _

_____

4.

large build

_ _ _ _ _   _ _ _ _ _

_____

5.

coffee cake

_ _ _ _ _ _   _ _ _ _

_____

6.

handcuffs

_ _ _ _ _ _ _ _ _

_____

7.

map

_ _ _

_____

8.

toolbox

_ _ _ _ _ _ _

_____

Glossary

burglar: a person who enters a place and steals things. _The burglar went into the store and stole six televisions._

employer: a person or business that another person works for. _The school is the employer of the teachers._

guilty: wrong, at fault. _The man was guilty of stealing a car._

lost: not knowing where someone or something is. _The child became lost because she did not follow directions._

on the house: free, paid for by business. _Her meal was on the house because it was her birthday._

suspect: a person others think is guilty. _The police took the suspect to the police station because they thought he stole some clothes._

10 Let the Buyer Beware

Victor Brashov worries about his business.
It is slow. A new customer, Barbara, comes
to the café. She offers to help Mr. Brashov.

How does Barbara help Mr. Brashov?

Who's in This Story?

Victor Brashov
the café owner

Barbara
a customer

Katherine
the waitress

Bill
a customer

Jamal
the handyman

Rosa
the cook

Jess
a regular customer

Henry
the busboy

1 Early Monday morning . . .

What's the problem Mr. Brashov?

Business is terrible! I don't understand why.

2 What did you do this weekend, Mr. Brashov?

On Saturday I cleaned my office. On Sunday I did paperwork.

3 Do you ever have fun?

I run a business here.

4 Why don't you date?

In Romania, men my age don't date.

5 The next day at the café . . .

What's the problem, Victor?

Why aren't there more people here?

6 Could I have another cup of coffee, please?

Sure.

That man spends more time here than I do.

7

8

9

10

11

12

13

14

15

16

17

18

19

✓ **Check Yourself**

3. What does Barbara tell Mr. Brashov?
   a. that his restaurant is charming
   b. that he is charming

4. What does Barbara ask Mr. Brashov?
   a. to pay the check
   b. to go to dinner

20

21

22

23

24

25 The waiter brings the check.

Victor, please. I will pay. You are my guest.

That is very kind of you. But I cannot allow a woman to pay for me.

26

27 A week later . . .

Victor is having a good time with Barbara.

I have a bad feeling about Barbara.

Relax. Let Victor enjoy himself.

28

✓ Check Yourself

5. What does Barbara say she can do for Mr. Brashov?

   a. help him get more customers

   b. help him get better food

6. How does Rosa feel about Barbara?

   a. She has a good feeling.

   b. She has a bad feeling.

29

30 Bill enters the café.

Will you have dinner with me tonight?

Well . . . I . . . I have children. It's not easy to get a babysitter.

31

32

33

She tells Bill about Mr. Brashov and Barbara.

34

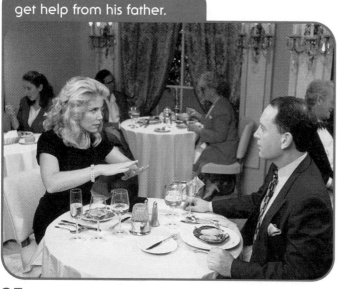

35

36

Bill and Katherine watch Barbara.

You need advertising.

I agree. I want your help. I'll write you a check.

37

Jamal comes to help. He gives Barbara and the man a dessert. He also takes a picture.

38

Jamal gives the film from the camera to Katherine.

39

✓ **Check Yourself**

7. What does Katherine see on her date with Bill?
   a. Barbara with Mr. Brashov
   b. Barbara with another man

8. Why is Jamal waiting table?
   a. He wants to work at Palmettos.
   b. He wants to take a picture of Barbara.

40

The next day Mr. Brashov sees the photos.

I don't understand.

This woman uses her good looks to take money from men.

I am a fool! I gave her $800.

41

What are we going to do?

She is probably miles away by now.

No, she is coming here tomorrow for more money.

42

43

Here is Bill. He can help us.

The next day at Crossroads Café . . .

Thank your father for letting me use his restaurant award.

He knows about people like Barbara. He is happy to help.

44

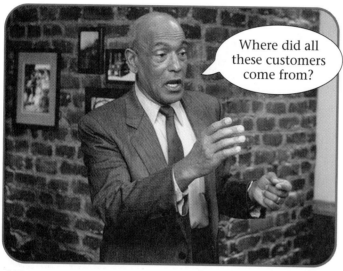

Where did all these customers come from?

45

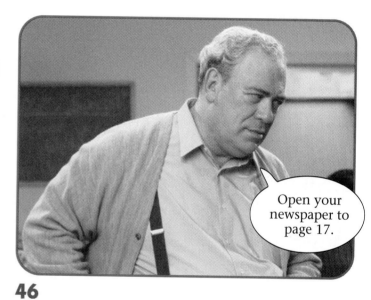

Open your newspaper to page 17.

46

Aah. Now I understand. Half off lunch special at Crossroads Café.

47

Here comes Barbara.

48

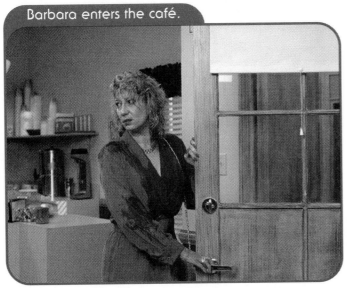

Barbara enters the café.

49

The newspaper just gave us an award for best new restaurant in the city. Excuse me a minute.

50

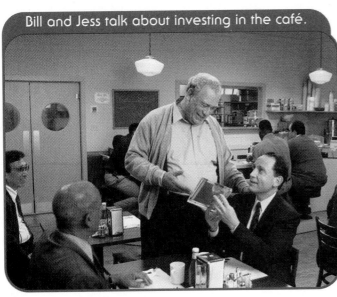

Bill and Jess talk about investing in the café.

51

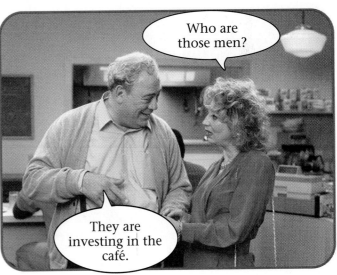

Who are those men?

They are investing in the café.

52

How much money are people investing?

$1600. Now I can pay you the $800 for promoting the café.

53

But I can invest in the café, too.

You have a deal.

54

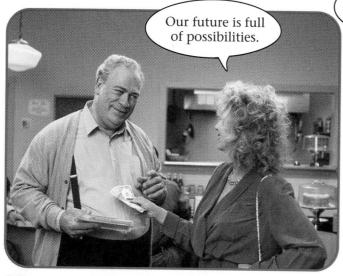

55 Our future is full of possibilities.

56 The only possibility is that I will call the police.

I don't understand.

Maybe this will help.

Mr. Brashov shows Barbara the picture Jamal took.

57

58 You fooled me.

59 I will never be such a fool again.

60

✓ **Check Yourself**

9. Why does Mr. Brashov think he is a fool?

   a. because Barbara isn't good looking

   b. because he gave Barbara money

10. Why does Mr. Brashov tell Barbara he will call the police?

    a. because she doesn't give him money

    b. because she took money from him

Tell the Story

Match the pictures with the sentences. Then tell the story to someone.

1.

2.

3.

4.

5.

6.

a. A few days later Katherine sees Barbara with another man.

b. Mr. Brashov gets his money back from Barbara.

c. A good-looking woman comes to the restaurant.

d. Jamal and Katherine show the photo to Mr. Brashov.

e. Barbara and Mr. Brashov go out to dinner.

f. Jamal takes a picture and gives the film to Katherine.

Search

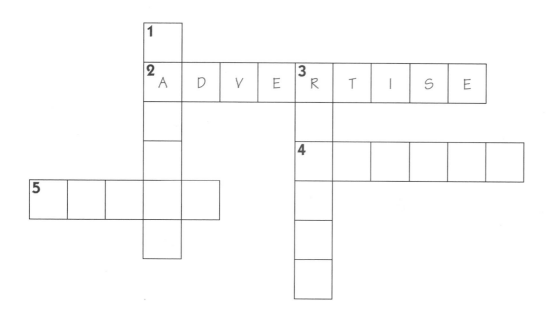

Complete the sentences. Then finish the puzzle above.

Across

2. Barbara helps restaurant owners find customers. She will _____ advertise _____ Crossroads Café.

4. Barbara sees Jess and Bill write _____ and give them to Mr. Brashov.

5. Palmettos has good service and very good food. The restaurant won an

_____ .

Down

1. Jamal takes a picture of Barbara. He uses his new _____ .

3. Barbara loves the dessert. She wants the _____ .

Build Your Vocabulary

An Elegant Restaurant

Read the words in the list. Find the numbers in the picture.

1. towel
2. champagne
3. napkin
4. tablecloth
5. knife
6. spoon
7. glasses
8. butter knife

Complete the sentences. Use the words from the picture.

1. Katherine will use the _____ knife (5) _____ next to her plate to cut food.

2. The knife is between Katherine's plate and a _____ for soup or ice cream.

3. To put butter on bread, she will use the _____ on the small plate.

4. The table is covered with a white _____.

5. The waiter has a white _____ over his arm.

6. Katherine put a _____ in her lap.

7. The waiter is showing Katherine and Bill a bottle of _____.

8. The waiter will pour the champagne into two of the _____.

Picture Dictionary

Study the picture and the English word. Copy the word. Then you may write the word in your language.

1.

award

<u>a w a r d</u>

_____

my language

2.

camera

_ _ _ _ _ _

_____

3.

check

_ _ _ _ _

_____

4.

check

_ _ _ _ _

_____

5.

film

_ _ _ _

_____

6.

photo

_ _ _ _ _

_____

Glossary

advertise: to announce to the public. *He wants to advertise in the newspaper, so he can get more customers.*

charming: pleasing and attractive. *She has a very charming smile and laugh.*

elegant: very, very nice. *She wears elegant clothes and jewelry.*

invest: to give money in order to make money. *He invested his money in a computer company.*

passed away: died. *My father had a heart attack. He passed away last year.*

sprinkler: a water system that protects buildings from fire. *Some buildings have sprinklers in their ceilings.*

11 No Vacancy

There's an apartment for rent in Katherine's building. Rosa applies for it, but she doesn't get it. The workers at the café decide to do something about it.

What do the workers do?

Who's in This Story?

Rosa
the café cook

Katherine
the waitress

Dorothy Walsh
Katherine's apartment
manager

Patty Peterson
a college student

Don Peterson
Patty's father

Jess
a regular customer

Victor Brashov
the café owner

Jamal
the handyman

Henry
the busboy and
a high school student

1

2

3

4

5

6

7 Henry has a new school project. Something about television news.

Henry in television?

8 Everybody is early this morning.

I ride with Katherine now. I don't have to worry about bus schedules.

9 I'm glad you're here, Rosa. I need to go over a supply list with you.

I'll just hang up my coat.

10 Rosa and Katherine go to their lockers.

I am so tired. The pipes in my apartment are noisy. I can't sleep.

Maybe you should move.

11 This morning I saw a *for rent* sign on your building. Maybe I should look at the apartment.

I'll give you the manager's phone number and you can call. You'll like Dorothy. She's a good friend.

12

✓ **Check Yourself**

1. Why is Henry looking for a videotape?
   a. He needs it for school.
   b. He wants Mr. Brashov to watch it.

2. Who is thinking about moving?
   a. Katherine
   b. Rosa

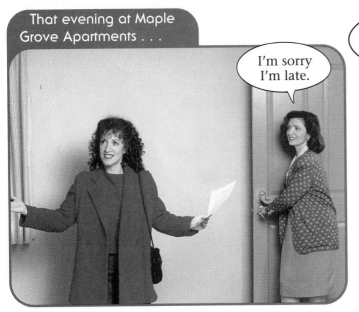

13 That evening at Maple Grove Apartments . . .

I'm sorry I'm late.

14 I love this apartment. It's the right size and the right price.

What is your name?

15 Rosa Rivera.

Well, Rosa. I'm Dorothy Walsh, the property manager.

It's a pleasure to meet you, Ms. Walsh.

16 Did you complete the rental application?

Yes. It's finished.

17 When will I know if I get the apartment?

Be patient. We have to process your application.

18 The next day at Crossroads Café . . .

The manual says the camera is easy to operate.

19

20

21

22

23

24

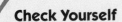

Check Yourself

3. Does Rosa like the apartment?

  a. No, it's too small.

  b. Yes, it's perfect.

4. What is Henry worried about?

  a. his work at the café

  b. a project for school

25

26

27

28

29

3011 No Vacancy ———— **179**

31

32

33

34

35

36

37

38

39

40

41

42

✓ **Check Yourself**

5. Why does Dorothy Walsh call the café?

   a. to tell Rosa that the apartment is rented

   b. to ask Katherine about Rosa

6. What does Patty think of the apartment?

   a. She wants to rent it now.

   b. She wants to look at some other places.

43

44

45

46

47

48

49

50

51

52

53

54

55

56

57

58

59

60

61 It's all here on tape.

62 I don't want this for my daughter. I want her to appreciate differences.

✓ Check Yourself

7. Who does Dorothy discriminate against?
   a. Rosa
   b. Patty

8. Why does the Crossroads Café staff go to the apartment?
   a. to rent an apartment
   b. to prove discrimination

63

64 You were wonderful.

Thank you, Rosa. But you still don't have this apartment.

65 Is that why you did this? For revenge? Because *chiquita* here didn't get the apartment?

Her name is Rosa. And she's my friend.

66 I thought we were friends.

Not any more, Dorothy. I'm going to continue living here. But you and I are no longer friends.

67

68

69

Later that day at the café . . .

70

71

72

Tell the Story

Match the picture with the sentence. Then tell the story to someone.

1.

2.

3.

4.

5.

6.

a. Henry gets it all on videotape.

b. Henry and Katherine begin the plan.

c. Rosa looks at an apartment.

d. Katherine discovers the apartment isn't rented.

e. Dorothy tells Rosa the apartment is rented.

f. Dorothy tells Mr. Brashov and Jess the apartment is rented to Patty.

Search

For each sentence in the box, write the number in a circle.

1. I didn't look at her application.

2. Sign here and your lovely daughter can move in.

3. The apartment is already rented.

4. It's a wonderful first apartment.

5. Be patient. We have to process your application.

6. Come back Saturday? That is fine.

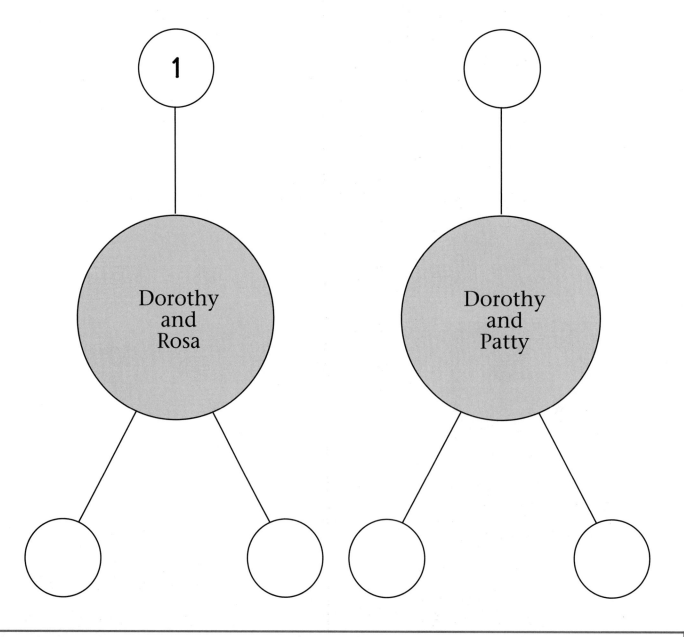

Build Your Vocabulary

Henry's Video Camera

Read the words in the list. Find the numbers in the picture.

1. handle
2. video camera
3. shoulder
4. lens cap
5. lens
6. button
7. instruction manual

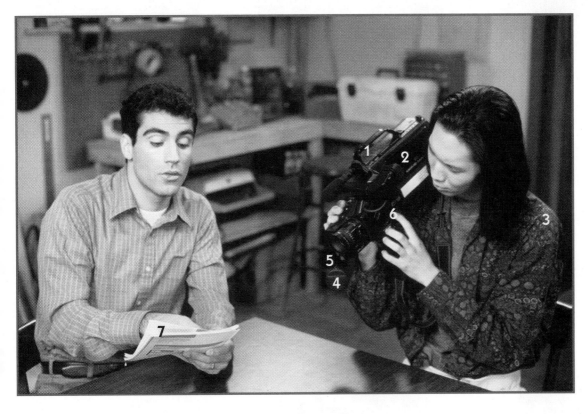

Complete the sentences. Use the words from the pictures.

1. Henry is learning how to use a ___video camera (2)___.

2. He is resting the camera on his _____.

3. Jamal is reading from the _____.

He reads the following:

4. To turn the camera on and off, push the _____.

5. Use the _____ when you pick up the camera.

6. Put on the _____ when you are not using the camera.

7. When the lens cap is on, you can't see through the _____.

Picture Dictionary

Study the picture and the English word. Copy the word. Then you may write the word in your language.

1.

anchorman

a n c h o r m a n

_ _ _ _ _ _ _ _ _

my language

2.

court

_ _ _ _ _

3.

judge

_ _ _ _ _

4.

lease

_ _ _ _ _

_____

5.

locker

_ _ _ _ _ _

6.

tape measure

_ _ _ _   _ _ _ _ _ _ _

7.

video camera

_ _ _ _ _   _ _ _ _ _ _

8.

videotape

_ _ _ _ _ _ _ _ _

Glossary

complaint: a statement of dissatisfaction about someone or something. *He filed a complaint against his landlord because there is no water or heat in his apartment.*

discriminate: to treat differently. *She thinks they didn't promote her because they discriminate against women.*

legal: permitted by law. *It is not legal to drink and drive.*

patient: calm, no hurry. *Children are not patient at Christmas. They want to open their presents right away.*

reference: a person who can make statements about another person's character. *Use him as a reference. He will say good things about you.*

revenge: hurting someone who has hurt you. *Her landlord kicked her out of the apartment, so she took revenge by leaving it very dirty.*

undesirables: people who are not wanted. *Some people think that homeless people are undesirables.*

12 Turning Points

Some people break in to Crossroads
Café. They make a mess and break many
things. The police look for the criminals
who did it.

What will the police discover?

Who's in This Story?

Victor Brashov
the café owner

Henry Chang
the delivery person
and busboy

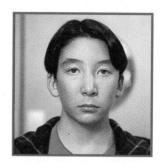

Edward Chang
Henry's younger
brother

Officer Rizzo
a police officer

Mrs. Chang
Henry and Edward's
mother

Johnny
a gang member

members of
the gang

neighborhood
people

Rosa
the cook

Katherine
the waitress

Jamal
the handyman

Jess
a regular customer

One morning at Crossroads Café . . .

1

2

3

4

Rosa is surprised. She says something in Spanish.

¿Que pasó aquí?

5

Let's check the back room.

No. Someone might still be in there.

6

7

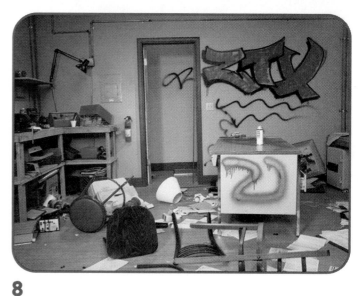

8

Mr. Brashov looks in his safe.

9

Mr. Brashov pulls the knife out of the wall.

10

11

12

✓ **Check Yourself**

1. What happened at the café?
   a. There is a fire.
   b. Somebody broke in.

2. What does Mr. Brashov find in the wall?
   a. a knife
   b. a picture

13

14

15

16

17

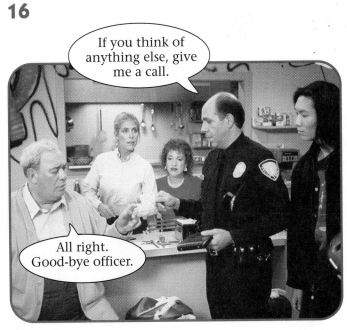

18

19

Rosa talks to Henry about the knife.

Henry, here's your knife.

Where was it?

In the back.

20

Mrs. Chang talks with Edward at their home. She is angry with him.

This is not the first time. If it happens again, you will be punished.

It's no big deal. I gave my work to the teacher the next day.

21

Henry comes into his bedroom.

Why were you late with your homework?

I had things to do.

22

Like what?

I don't know. Just things.

23

Henry throws the knife at the dartboard.

24

25

26

27

28

29

30

Jess comes into the café.

Jess, Rosa needs a car. But she doesn't know how to drive.

Rosa, driving is easy. I can teach you.

31

Later that day . . .

This is easy.

32

33

✓ **Check Yourself**

5. Why is Mrs. Chang angry with Edward?
   a. He doesn't clean his room.
   b. He has problems with his school work.

6. What is Rosa's problem?
   a. She doesn't have enough money to buy a car.
   b. She doesn't know how to drive.

34

At the Chang house . . .

Hey.

Hi.

35

Why was this knife at Crossroads Café?

I don't know.

36

37

Henry sees bruises on Edward.

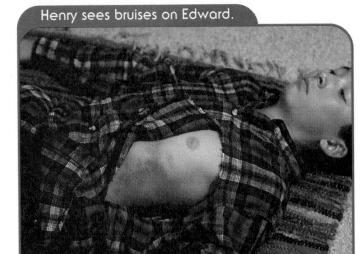

38

Where did you get the bruises?

I fell down at school.

39

Yeah, right. If you don't want to talk to me about this . . . . You can talk to Mom.

Wait! . . . Every day, they are messing with me.

40

What are you talking about? Who?

The gang. First, they wanted money. Then I had to break in to the restaurant.

41

Why do you want to join a gang?

If I don't join, they will beat me again.

42

43

Why didn't you tell me?

I wanted to take care of it myself.

44

The next day at the café . . .

45

Rosa, you want to make a left turn. What do you do?

I put out my arm like this.

46

O.K. There is a traffic light ahead. Put your foot on the brake.

What brake?

47

✓ **Check Yourself**

7. Why does Edward have a lot of bruises?

   a. A gang is beating him up.

   b. He fell down at school.

8. Who teaches Rosa to drive?

   a. Mr. Brashov

   b. Jamal

48

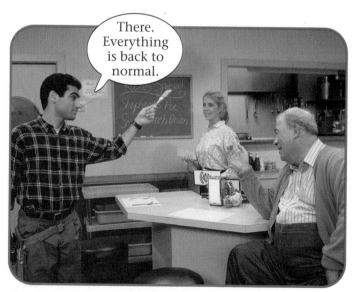

There. Everything is back to normal.

49

50

51

52

53

54

55

I'm going to take this boy to the police station. He needs to learn a lesson.

Wait. I have a plan to stop this gang.

56

That night at the Chang's . . .

Did you call Johnny yet?

Yeah. I'm going to meet him at eight o'clock tomorrow night.

57

Late the next evening, the gang comes into the café.

Where did you get the key?

I stole it from my brother.

58

O.K., now, where is the safe?

It's in the back.

59

Hey, what's going on? Get out of my way!

No.

60

You can't stop all of us by yourself.

61

62

63

64

65

66

67

68

69

70

71

72

✓ **Check Yourself**

9. What happens to the gang members?
   a. The people in the neighborhood stop them.
   b. They break in to another restaurant.

10. How does Edward pay for the damages?
    a. He gets money from his mother.
    b. He works for Mr. Brashov.

Tell the Story

Put the pictures and sentences in order. Number 1 to 6. Then tell the story to someone.

_____ a.

The police ask some questions
at the café.

_____ b.

Mr. Brashov finds a knife
in the wall.

_____ c.

The police take the gang
members to jail.

_____ d.

Edward tells Henry about
the gang.

1 e.

Someone breaks in to the café.

_____ f.

People in the neighborhood
stop the gang.

Search

Unscramble the word. Complete the sentence.

1. Mr. Brashov looks in the _____safe_____ for his money. (e s f a)

2. Jamal tells Rosa to put both hands on the _____. (s g e r e t n i   w l e h e)

3. The colors of the _____ are red, yellow and green. (f c i t a r f   l g i t h)

4. Jamal has to buy two cans of _____ for the walls of the café. (a n p t i)

5. The police want the _____ of the criminals. (i t s p f g r i n r e n)

6. Sometimes people write _____ on walls and buildings. (i g i f a f r t)

Now find each word below. When you find a word, circle it.

```
W  T  R  A  F  F  I  C  L  I  G  H  T  N
E  F  I  N  G  E  R  P  R  I  N  T  S  C
B  A  A  V  U  Q  L  A  P  R  O  N  A  D
G  R  A  F  F  I  T  I  R  Z  Y  T  F  F
X  S  T  E  E  R  I  N  G  W  H  E  E  L
A  I  E  P  L  M  O  T  D  C  P  O  N  B
```

Build Your Vocabulary

Henry and Edward's Bedroom

Read the words in the list. Find the numbers in the picture.

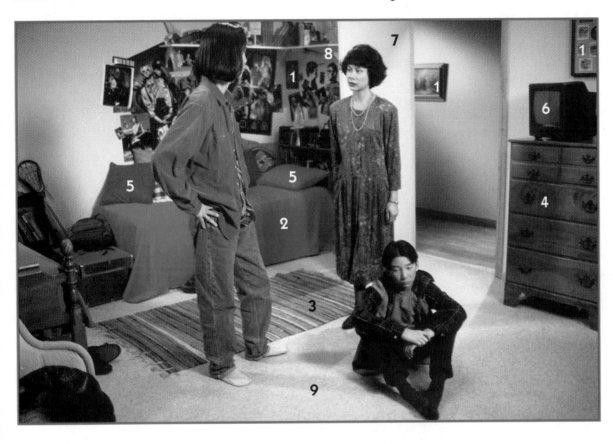

1. pictures
2. bed
3. rug
4. dresser
5. pillows
6. television
7. door
8. shelf
9. carpet

Complete the sentences. Use the words from the picture.

1. Edward is sitting on the _____*carpet (9)*_____ in his room.

2. There are many _____ on the bed in the room.

3. Edward sleeps in his _____ at night.

4. The boys put things on the _____ over one of the beds.

5. Henry and Edward put a lot of _____ on the wall.

6. When Henry or Edward want to be alone, they close the bedroom _____.

7. Edward and Henry often watch _____ at night.

8. The television is on top of a wooden _____.

9. A colorful _____ is on top of the carpet.

Picture Dictionary

Study the picture and the English word. Copy the word. Then you may write the word in your language.

1.

dartboard

_d a r t b o a r d_

my language

2.

fingerprints

3.

graffiti

4.

knife

5.

paint

6.

safe

7.

spray paint

8.

traffic light

Glossary

break in to: to enter a house or building by force. *The criminal likes to break in to houses of rich people.*

bruises: black and blue marks on the body after an injury such as a beating or a fall. *The woman has bruises on her face because of the car accident.*

damage: harm or injury to something. *The storm does a lot of damage to the trees in the town.*

gang: a group of people who work together, sometimes to commit crimes. *There was a fight between two gangs from different parts of the city.*

13 Trading Places

Change is everywhere. The workers at Crossroads Café change jobs. Carol and Jess change roles.

What do they learn from the changes?

Who's in This Story?

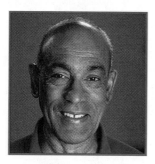

Jess Washington
retired, a regular customer
at the café

Carol Washington
Jess's wife, who works

Rosa
the cook

Henry
the delivery person

Jamal
the handyman

Victor Brashov
the café owner

Katherine
the waitress

1 It is closing time at Crossroads Café.

2 Mr. Brashov is having something to eat.

I asked for a hamburger and french fries.

But fish and fresh vegetables are better for you.

3 That is a big fish.

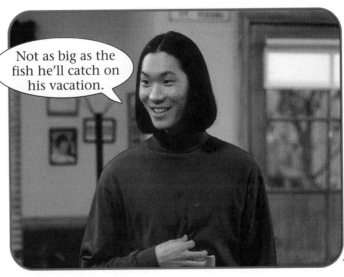

4 Not as big as the fish he'll catch on his vacation.

5 The fish I'm going to catch will be *this* big.

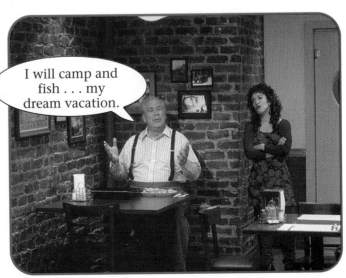

6 I will camp and fish . . . my dream vacation.

7

Jamal enters the dining area.

Jamal, what happened?

The pipe leaks.

8

A delivery man enters the restaurant.

Where's the rice?

What rice?

9

Jess, How can I take a vacation? How can Crossroads Café get along without me?

10

Mr. Brashov doesn't think we can manage the café.

11

12

It is night at Jess and Carol's house.

Hi, honey.

13

14

15

16

17

18

19

✓ **Check Yourself**

3. Why isn't Jess happy about the watch?

a. He says they can't afford it.

b. He says he doesn't need it.

4. Why does Mr. Brashov want the workers to trade jobs?

a. because someone may get sick

b. because someone may quit

20

21

It is night at Jess and Carol's house.

How was work?

Crazy. I hope you didn't start dinner. I want to try a new restaurant.

But it's not Saturday. We only eat out on Saturday.

Now that I'm working, we can afford to eat out more often.

22

No, we can't. Look at these bills.

23

I know. I paid some of them last night.

You what? Why did you do that?

24

25

26

27

28

29

30

31

32

33

34

35

✓ Check Yourself

5. Where does Carol want to eat dinner?

  a. at home

  b. in a restaurant

6. Why do Jess and Carol argue about the bills?

  a. because Carol paid some of them

  b. because Carol didn't pay any of them

36

The next day at Crossroads Café . . .

How did things go with Carol last night?

She was asleep when I got home.

37

As Victor and Jess play chess, the workers start their new jobs.

38

Katherine cooks.

39

Henry waits tables.

40

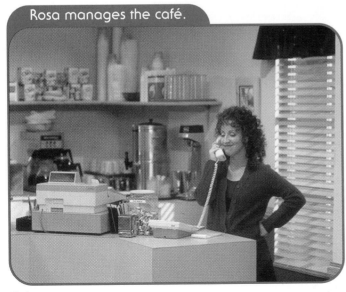

Rosa manages the café.

41

Jamal makes deliveries.

42

43

Victor, your experiment is working.

We will know soon. The lunch crowd will be here soon.

44

Five, four, three, two, one . . .

The lunch crowd arrives.

45

Katherine and Henry look worried.

46

Katherine works as fast as she can.

47

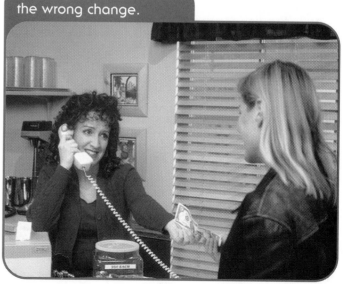

Rosa gives a customer the wrong change.

48

Henry drops a customer's food.

49

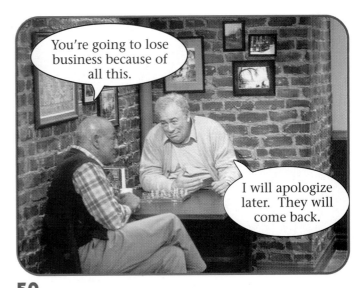

You're going to lose business because of all this.

I will apologize later. They will come back.

50

51

Carol visits Jess at the café.

Why aren't you at work?

I'm on my lunch break. I wanted to see how you were doing.

52

Something is different about this place.

It's Victor's experiment. He wanted everyone to switch jobs for a day.

53

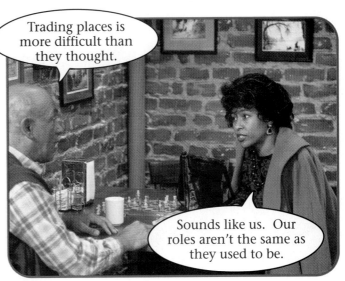

Trading places is more difficult than they thought.

Sounds like us. Our roles aren't the same as they used to be.

54

55 You mean because you're working and I'm not?

More than that, it's about change, and change is not easy.

56 The watch is very handsome. I'm glad you didn't return it.

57 Jamal comes back from a delivery.

Hello?

58 There is no need to yell, Mrs. Johnson.

59 Mr. Brashov? Katherine, call 911!

60

✓ **Check Yourself**

9. How are Carol and Jess's roles different?
   a. He works and buys her things now, but he didn't used to.
   b. She works and buys him things now, but she didn't used to.

10. What does Carol say about change?
    a. It is easy.
    b. It is not easy.

Tell the Story

Put the pictures and sentences in order. For each story, number 1 to 3. Then tell each story to someone.

Jess and Carol's Story

_____ a.

Carol and Jess have a fight.

__1__ b.

Carol gives Jess a present.

_____ c.

Jess tells Mr. Brashov
about the fight with Carol.

The Workers' Story

_____ a.

At first the experiment works.

_____ b.

The workers have trouble in their new jobs.

_____ c.

Mr. Brashov decides to try an experiment.

Search

Look at the picture. Read the sentence. Circle Yes or No.

1. **Look at Picture 2**
    Rosa says fish and vegetables are better for Mr. Brashov than hamburger and french fries.

    2

    (YES)   NO

2. **Look at Picture 13**
    Carol bought Jess a gift because it's Jess's birthday.

    13

    YES   NO

3. **Look at Picture 39**
    Katherine is usually the waitress. Today, she is the cook.

    39

    YES   NO

4. **Look at Picture 40**
    Henry is usually the delivery person. Today, he is the manager.

    40

    YES   NO

5. **Look at Picture 42**
    Jamal makes deliveries.

    42

    YES   NO

6. **Look at Picture 59**
    Mr. Brashov is a sick man.

    59

    YES   NO

Build Your Vocabulary

Jess and Carol's Living Room

Read the words in the list. Find the numbers in the picture.

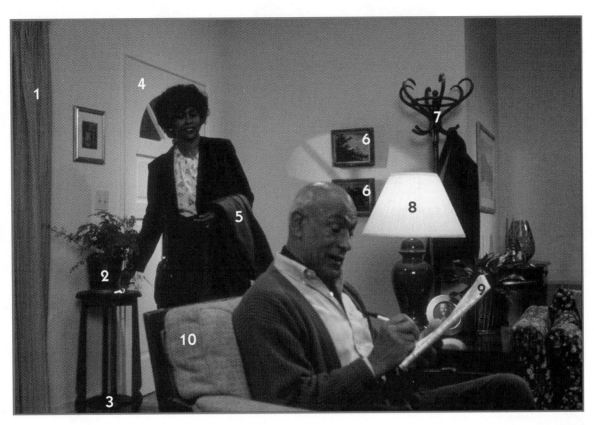

1. curtain
2. plant
3. plant stand
4. door
5. coat
6. pictures
7. coat rack
8. table lamp
9. newspaper
10. easy chair

Complete the sentences. Use the words from the picture.

1. Carol is standing in front of the _____ *door (4)* _____.

2. She is carrying her _____.

3. Her right hand is resting on a _____.

4. On top of the plant stand there is a _____.

5. Two _____ are on the wall to the left of the coat rack.

6. Carol's husband Jess is sitting in an _____.

7. He is holding a _____.

8. It is dark, but he can see because the _____ is on.

9. Behind the table lamp there is a _____.

10. It is night, so the window _____ is closed.

Picture Dictionary

Study the picture and the English word. Copy the word. Then you may write the word in your language.

1.

$$2 + 2 = 4$$

add

<u>a</u> <u>d</u> <u>d</u>

_____

my language

2.

camp

— — — —

_____

3.

drop

— — — —

_____

4.

fish

— — — —

_____

5.

gift

— — — —

_____

6.

$$10 - 2 = 8$$

subtract

— — — — — — — —

_____

7.

watch

— — — — —

_____

Glossary

afford: to have the money to buy something or to do something. *Henry can afford to rent a tuxedo.*

argue: to fight. *Brothers and sisters often argue about toys.*

crowd: many people. *There is always a crowd when a store has a sale.*

experiment: trying something new. *Rosa's special is often an experiment.*

leak: lose water. *The glass leaks, so the table is wet.*

switch: change or exchange; trade. *Sisters often like to switch clothes.*

Teacher/Tutor Appendix

If you have read the section *To the Learner* at the beginning of this book, the information in this appendix will provide a more detailed understanding of the scope and the goals of the program. The *Crossroads Café* print and video materials are closely correlated to provide everything needed for successful, non-stressful language-learning experiences, either alone or with a teacher or tutor.

The *Worktexts*

The two *Crossroads Café Worktexts* provide multi-level language activities with three levels of challenge: Beginning High, Intermediate Low and Intermediate High (or SPL 4, 5, and 6). These activities are visually designated in the *Worktext* as ✪, ✪✪, or ✪✪✪, respectively. The 1-star exercises ask learners to communicate using words and phrases; responses are frequently based on a visual stimulus. The 2-star exercises ask learners to communicate using learned phrases and structures; responses may be based on visual stimulus or text. The 3-star exercises are designed for students who can participate in basic conversation; responses are most often based on text not visuals. Every *Worktext* unit contains exercises designed to develop *story comprehension, language skills,* and *higher order thinking* and to provide practice in reading, writing, and speaking. Every *Worktext* unit opens with a photo depicting the theme of the storyline, a list of learning objectives, and a learning strategy.

Crossroads Café Worktext Framework

	Exercise Section	Purpose	✪	✪✪	✪✪✪
Story Comprehension (Video)	*Before You Watch*	Preview story-line vocabulary and events.	Match words with video photos to highlight key plot points.	Match sentences with photos.	Write a question about each photo.
	Focus for Watching	Provide story focus.	Answer questions about elements of main plot.	Answer additional questions about main plot.	Answer additional questions focused on details of story.
	After You Watch	Check story comprehension.	Answer yes/no questions about the story plot using same content as previous two exercises.	Arrange 3–6 sentences about story in proper sequence.	Add, in the appropriate place, 3–4 new sentences providing additional detail.
Language Development	*Your New Language*	Focus on language function and grammatical structure of the "Word Play" video segment, e.g., making promises: *I promise to. . ., I promise that I will. . . .*	Copy words or phrases into sentences conveying language functions.	Match 2 parts of 2-line exchanges, e.g., question-answer, statement-response.	Complete a fill-in-the-blank dialogue with correct grammatical structures.

	Exercise Section	Purpose	★	★★	★★★
	Discourse Exercise	Enable learners to see language flow.	Sequence a dialogue of 3–4 sentences.	Sequence a dialogue of 4–6 sentences.	Sequence a dialogue of 6–8 sentences.
	In Your Community	Develop reading skills using reading materials from the community, e.g., a lease.	Answer factual questions taken directly from reading.	Answer factual questions requiring synthesis.	Answer questions requiring inference.
	Read and Write	Develop reading skills	Identify main idea.	Identify factual details.	Identify tone or feeling.
		Determine meaning from context.	Identify words/phrases with same meaning.	Identify words/phrases that are clues to meaning.	Infer word meaning from text clues.
		Develop writing skills.	Provide basic factual information.	Provide additional detail.	Draw conclusions, express opinions, and other analysis, synthesis, and evaluation tasks.
Thinking Skills	*What Do You Think?*	Express and support opinions.	Indicate opinions by matching or selecting from multiple-choice items.	React to characters' opinions.	Write sentences expressing and supporting your opinions.
	Culture Clips	Recall key information presented in the *Culture Clips* video segment.	Match art with sentences from the culture clip video segment.	Complete fill-in-the-blank passage on culture clip concepts.	Respond to a situation or express an opinion related to culture clip theme.
	Check Your English	Demonstrate new material mastery.	Match written words with art depicting vocabulary.	Copy words to form a sentence/question using grammatical structure(s) presented in *Your New Language*.	Complete fill-in-the-blank passage that provides a story summary.

The *Photo Stories*

The *Photo Stories* have two primary purposes:

- They serve as a preview activity for viewers with beginning-low (but not literacy-level) English proficiency by assisting them in following the main story line when they view the video. The high-success, low-stress follow-up activities in the Photo Stories are ideal motivators for this group of learners, most of whom could not access the story without this special help.

- They can be used with learners at higher levels to preview and review the story line.

The diagram below and the descriptions that follow illustrate the carefully designed, yet simple and predictable structure of the *Photo Story* episodes.

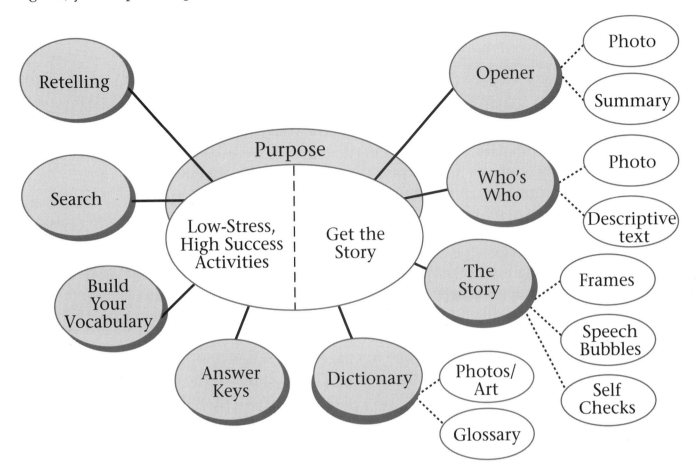

As the diagram suggests, the *Photo Stories* have a limited number of basic components, or elements:

1. **The Unit Opener:** This component helps the learner focus, using a large photo (the same one that appears at the beginning of each *Worktext* unit) that captures the theme of the episode and a capsulized summary statement of only 3 to 5 sentences that provides an overview without giving away the outcome.

2. **Who's Who:** Photos of the characters in the episode that are key to the main story line are included here. Below each photo is the character's name and a phrase describing something about the person that relates to this particular episode. For example, for Katherine in the episode "Family Matters," the phrase reads, "A single mother of two."

3. **The Story:** The story is told with photos from the episode and text, using frames and speech bubbles. Included at appropriate intervals throughout the sequence of frames are comprehension questions with which the student can self-check his or her success at "making meaning." The language "spoken" by the characters in the frames is that heard in the videos, but it is frequently simplified by deleting information, structures, and words.

4. **The Dictionary:** The dictionary provides learners with a resource for clarifying words they do not understand. It has two parts—visuals and glossary. The visuals—photos or art—may be objects, emotions, or actions that can be visually portrayed. The glossary contains six or fewer words that learners encounter in the frames. These words are not easily depicted visually and may require some explanation. The definitions given are very brief and simple. In addition, for each word in the glossary, a sentence other than the one in the video story is provided to model usage.

5. **The Activity Pages:** There are three types of activity pages—Retelling, Searches, and Build Your Vocabulary. In the Retelling activities, learners sequence pictures that represent key elements in the story. The Searches check comprehension of more detailed information, but still focus on the main theme or story line. Answers may be based on text and photo, photo only, or text only. In Build Your Vocabulary, the exercises center around a large picture that shows a scene from the story. The scene selected is rich in vocabulary that is useful to learners but not crucial to the main plot. Items in the picture are numbered, and a vocabulary list keyed to the numbers is provided. Below the pictures and vocabulary list, a series of sentences with blanks in them provides opportunities for learners to put each word into context.

6. **The Answer Keys:** The answers to all activity pages are printed upside down at the bottom of the page on which the exercise falls. The exception is the **Check Yourself** comprehension questions, whose answers are grouped together on the bottom of the first activity page.

In this way, through a well-designed combination of pictures, text, and language-learning activities, the *Photo Stories* teach basic language and reading-comprehension skills—thus propelling beginning low ESL learners toward higher levels of understanding and fluency.

Teacher's Resource Books

To help classroom teachers and distance-learning instructors give students all the help they need, each of the two *Crossroads Café Teacher's Resource Books* provides general directions for how to work with the program and specific instructions for how to use each episode. Each also has 52 reproducible master activities—4 for each of the 13 episodes in the book—for teachers to copy and give to students to complete in pairs and small groups. By working through these activities, students will be able to engage one another interactively. The following pages are examples of the type of guidance for teachers and activities for students that the *Teacher's Resource Books* provide. With these tools, teachers can make the most effective use of the *Crossroads Café* program during class time.

In Your Community

Bring to class the help wanted ads from a variety of newspapers for additional practice in reading such ads. Review them first to make sure there are ads for food servers (waiters/waitresses), bus/delivery persons, and handymen. Then do the following:

- Divide learners into mixed ability groups and distribute at least one newspaper to each group. Give each group a felt tip marker, plain white paper, scissors, and tape or glue.
- Assign each group a job classification. Ask the groups to look through their newspapers and circle all the help wanted ads for their job classification.
- Have groups compare the ads they circled to the one (for their category) in the worktext.
- Have learners cut out the ad that is most like the one in their worktexts, label it, and mount it on the plain paper.
- Have learners cut out the ads that appeal to them most, label them, and mount them on the plain paper.
- Have learners underline, with the marker, all the similarities to the worktext help wanted ad. Each group should then select one person to report to the class.

Read And Write

Visit a card shop. See how many different kinds of *I'm sorry* cards there are. Bring a few cards to class to share with the learners. Pass the cards around or make overhead transparencies before learners write the note in the worktext. Also remind learners they do not have to share anything too personal. If they cannot think of a note of apology, they can make up something.

If possible, replay the video scenes below that feature Jess and Carol before learners complete the writing activities in the worktext.

Counter Times	Scenes
01:65–02:29	Carol gives Jess a watch.
04:15–05:08	Jess and Carol argue about going out for dinner.
08:05–08:60	Carol comes to the café to talk to Jess.

Extension Activity #1 is a large group discussion about making apologies.

- Talk about Jess and Carol's arguments in the video—the watch and going out to dinner. Talk about Jess's note to Carol.
- Ask learners what they do when they are sorry or want to apologize for something. Tell them:
  Raise your hand if you ever say you're sorry.
  Raise your hand if you ever write a note to say you're sorry.
  Raise your hand if you ever send flowers to say you're sorry.
- Ask learners about other things they do when they apologize. Write them down for everyone to see. If you observe any gender or cultural patterns, point them out and ask the learners to comment.

Extension Activity #2 is a roleplay. Prepare situation cards such as the ones below. Here are some suggestions:

- You're late to class (student/teacher).
- You forgot to meet your friend for lunch (friend/friend).
- You forgot to tell your spouse you'd be home late (wife/husband).
- You forgot your friend's birthday (friend/friend).
- You were playing music too loud (neighbor/neighbor).

A variation is to have learners think of situations with a partner and write them on blank 3" × 5" cards. Collect the cards. Ask for volunteers to roleplay each situation. Each pair picks a card at random and decides which roles each will play.

What Do You Think?

The employees traded jobs and Carol and Jess traded roles. After learners complete this page in the worktext, have them do a three-step interview on the theme of the unit—Trading Places. Ask the following questions.

32   Crossroads Café   English Learning Program

Handout 13-A

Work with a partner. One person is **A** and the other is **B**. Work together to complete the grid below.

1. In the *top left-hand box*, write **four** things you both can do well.
2. In the *top right-hand box*, write **four** things **A** can do but **B** can't.
3. In the *bottom left-hand box* write **four** things **B** can do but **A** can't.
4. In the *bottom right-hand box* write **four** things neither of you can do well.

Both A and B	Only A
Only B	Neither A nor B

34   Crossroads Café   English Learning Program   © 1996 Heinle & Heinle Publishers

---

The Crossroads Café Partner's Guide

The *Partner's Guide* is a small book—just 32 pages—that a formal tutor, a relative, a friend, a coworker, or a neighbor can use to help a learner improve his or her English. This little guide explains, in simple, direct language, what the "helper" can do to make learning with each episode of *Crossroads Café* even better for the student. The guide provides one page of special instructions for each episode, as well as some general suggestions for a predictable yet lively approach to working with the learner. People who have never taught and seasoned tutors will find a wealth of hints in the *Partner's Guide* for helping students succeed with their English.

The Crossroads Café Reproducible Master Packet

For the tutor who is working with more than one learner of *Crossroads Café*, the same 104 reproducible masters that are part of the *Teacher's Resource Books* are available separately. The masters can also be used by tutors who want to maximize a single learner's opportunities for interaction by working through the communicative activities in a learning-partner role with the student.

Index